SOCIAL
ROMANTICISM
IN FRANCE
1830–1848

Thinkers are but the scouts of humanity along the unknown paths of the future. It is true that they break the trail, but mankind never travels by the precise way they have prescribed: it takes upon itself to make the break-through which best suits its multiple designs

PECQUEUR, *Économie sociale*, ii. 402

SOCIAL
ROMANTICISM
IN FRANCE

1830–1848

WITH A SELECTIVE
CRITICAL BIBLIOGRAPHY

DAVID OWEN EVANS
D.LITT. (OXON.)

019906

1969
OCTAGON BOOKS
New York

Originally published 1951 by Oxford University Press

Reprinted 1969
by special arrangement with Oxford University Press

OCTAGON BOOKS
A DIVISION OF FARRAR, STRAUS & GIROUX, INC.
19 Union Square West
New York, N. Y. 10003

AM

LIBRARY OF CONGRESS CATALOG CARD NUMBER: 77-96180

Printed in U.S.A. by
TAYLOR PUBLISHING COMPANY
DALLAS, TEXAS

CONTENTS

019906

ABBREVIATIONS

Archiv	*Archiv für das Studium der neueren Sprachen*
CIS	*Cahiers internationaux de sociologie*
JHI	*Journal of the History of Ideas*
JPE	*Journal of Political Economy*
MF	*Mercure de France*
MLN	*Modern Language Notes*
MLR	*Modern Language Review*
NL	*Nouvelles Littéraires*
NRF	*Nouvelle Revue Française*
PMLA	*Publications of the Modern Language Association of America*
RB	*Revue bleue*
RC	*Revue critique d'histoire et de littérature*
RDM	*Revue des Deux Mondes*
Rhist	*Revue historique*
RHES	*Revue d'histoire économique et sociale*
RHL	*Revue d'histoire littéraire de la France*
RIS	*Revue internationale de sociologie*
RLC	*Revue de littérature comparée*
RPar	*Revue de Paris*
Rph	*Revue philosophique*
RScPol	*Revue des sciences politiques*
RSoc	*Revue socialiste*
RSH	*Revue de synthèse historique*
SP	*Studies in Philology*
TLS	*Times Literary Supplement*
ZFSL	*Zeitschrift für französische Sprache und Litteratur*
s.d.	*no date*
Diss.	*Dissertation*

SOCIAL ROMANTICISM IN FRANCE

VIEWED in the perspective of these stormy days, how orderly and peaceful life seems to have been in the thirties of the nineteenth century!

The horizon was not heavy with alarms; each change of wind did not bring with it new fears; there was confidence in the present and even in the future, so that, one hundred years ago, the business of living was easier than it is today.... The grapes had ripened under happy skies, and people put away in their cellars wine they were sure of drinking.... The 5 per cent. stock stood at 107 fr. 90 and the 4 per cent. at 98 fr. 50, like a barometer at set fair. The middle classes had government securities in their safety-deposit boxes, and in their pockets golden louis.... A deputy proclaimed from the rostrum of the Chamber: 'We are enjoying a period of profound peace.'[1]

Many contemporaries of the Romantic poets would have agreed that they lived in a pleasant and happy era. The government of King Louis-Philippe, described by Thiers and Guizot as 'the best of republics', appeared to some a kind of golden age. And it is true that Europe in 1835 enjoyed great benefits which we have lost. A peace, arbitrarily imposed, had been successfully defended for a generation. Industry and commerce were expanding, wages were paid in honest metal, and the British income tax was not nine shillings in the pound. There were great achievements also in the arts and sciences. Berlioz, Delacroix, Liszt, Chopin, Michelet, Lamartine, Auguste Comte, Sainte-Beuve, Geoffroy Saint-Hilaire, Stendhal, Victor Hugo, Balzac, Musset, Alfred de Vigny: these great names

[1] P. Hazard, 'Il y a cent ans', *RDM*, 15 October 1935.

of the France of 1835 were still great names in 1935, and this too is a standard by which we estimate a society and a civilization.

But there is another side to the picture. France in those days was not nearly as sure of herself as she seemed to be. Sainte-Beuve, whose sociological notations are extremely trustworthy, characterizes the prevailing atmosphere as one of social frustration.[1] The most memorable work of art of the year was Daumier's masterpiece *La Rue Transnonain*. The scene, a workman's lodgings, is a shambles. On the floor, in a pool of blood, lies the body of a man murdered in bed. Beneath him is his dead child, and the dark background seems to hide a woman's body. The massacre of April 1834 was motivated by fear of the infant trade-union movement. Forty thousand troops were mobilized, and in a single house in this street twelve innocent people were butchered in cold blood. The same year Daumier published a second lithograph, showing a young Republican in irons in a prison cell. Watching him is the Attorney-General, but the workman's eyes are fixed on another figure, visible only to him, a female figure in a Phrygian cap advancing in a halo of light. And under the picture the artist has written: *Et pourtant elle marche!* 'With the world began a struggle which shall end with the world, and not sooner—the struggle of man against nature, of mind against matter, of freedom against fate. History is nothing other than the relation of that interminable warfare. . . . Freedom doubtless has its limitations, *and yet it moves*, as Galileo says.'[2] Such are the social realities, grotesque and sublime, of 1834–5. Writing in the *Revue des Deux Mondes* of a hundred years ago, Chateaubriand,

---

[1] *Portraits contemporains*, i. 244 n. (1834).
[2] Michelet, *Introduction à l'histoire universelle* (Hachette, 1831), 9–10.

politically the most conservative of the writers of that generation, gives this description of the contemporary scene:

Europe is racing towards democracy. . . . France and England, like two enormous battering-rams, beat again and again upon the crumbling ramparts of the old society. The most audacious doctrines concerning property, equality, and liberty are proclaimed night and morning in the face of monarchs trembling behind a triple guard of unreliable soldiers. . . .

A society in which individuals may possess incomes of two millions while others are reduced to living in hovels on heaps of decayed matter alive with worms, . . . can such a society remain stationary on such foundations in the midst of the advance of ideas?. . . What the new society will be I know not; I no more understand it than the ancients could understand the slaveless society born of Christianity. How fortunes will be levelled, how wages will be equalized with labour, how womanhood will attain complete emancipation, I do not know. Presumably the *human species* will grow in stature, but it is to be feared that the individual *man* may decline, certain eminent faculties of genius be lost, and imagination, poetry, and the arts perish in the cells of a hive-society in which each individual will be nothing more than a bee, a cog in a machine, an atom in organized matter. . . .

Modern society has taken ten centuries to establish, and now is in process of decomposition. . . . This declining world will recover its energies only when that process has reached its final stage, whereafter society will begin to ascend to a new level of life.[1]

The figures for the population of France during the Monarchy of July reflect graphically the accelerating transformation of an agricultural country into an industrial.[2]

---

[1] 'Avenir du monde', published by Sainte-Beuve in *RDM*, 15 April 1834, from Chateaubriand's *Mémoires d'Outre-tombe*.

[2] Urban population (1830) 15 per cent., (1846) 25 per cent. of the total—Charléty, *La Monarchie de Juillet*, 210–11.

The Romantic period in French literature is, in French life, the age of the industrial revolution.

In England, a growth of the urban population by nearly $31\frac{1}{2}$ per cent. had already taken place during the years 1811–31, and was followed by a further 50 per cent. increase at cities like Birmingham, Manchester, and Sheffield. Heavy industry reached a high pitch of activity in Great Britain during the eighteen-thirties. France, on the other hand, was still predominantly an agricultural country; a great historical process was just setting in. Industry during the Restoration period had remained, as during the Empire, mainly based on rural craftsmanship. Few factories were built, and the total steel capacity of the country in 1827 was only 5,485 tons.[1] The July Monarchy (1830–48) is the period at which the French economy is creating its first heavy industries and transport system, draining off capital in a vast initial outlay profitable only to a later generation, and imposing strains and stresses on the nation generally which, for various reasons, were to be prolonged until about 1870. The feature of the period is the progress of mechanization; and its human cost was great, as it had proved in England and was later to do in Russia. The immediate result of the introduction of spinning-looms, steam machinery, and machine tools was that rural craftsmen were thrown out of work. So many left the poverty-stricken countryside for the towns, attracted by the prospects held out to them of work and wages, and little suspecting the periods of unemployment, depression, and wage-reductions that awaited them, that an unprecedented housing shortage developed at industrial centres such as Lille and Rouen. The solution found was the slum. No unemployment figures were kept in Louis-Philippe's reign, but we know that in 1832,

[1] Sée, *La Vie économique en France sous la Monarchie censitaire*, 53, 77.

for instance, one-seventh of the population of Paris was dependent on charity. In 1831 the sufferings of the silk-workers (*les canuts*) at Lyons led to armed revolt following the laying-off of hands by the silk-factories and the reduction of wages to 18 sous for the eighteen-hour day. 'The struggle henceforth is between those who have and those who have not', comments a contemporary economist.[1] Another more violent outbreak occurred there in April 1834. 'What sort of society is this?', asks a retired Captain of Engineers writing on 14 June under the direct impression of these events, 'this society which summons to one point thousands of men, and tells them: "Come, the workshops are open; here are wages for you and your children"; trains them to do a certain kind of work, and then, having *mechanized*[2] them, and encircled them within the iron ring of a determined fate, says to them: "Now we can pay you only half-wages, quarter-wages, or no wage at all, for there is no more work for you . . ." What manner of society is this?'[3]

The Lyons riots of 1831 and 1834 are clear signs of social revolution. Since Waterloo wages had steadily declined. A statistician of the period estimates that from 1816 to 1840 they fell by 25 per cent.[4] The average wage of the French working man in the early eighteen-thirties was about 2 francs a day or between 492 and 587 francs a year, and many earned less. But in 1832 a minimum of 760 francs, some say 860 francs, a year was needed to keep an average working-class family from starvation.[5] Only a third of the French population was able to afford meat. Eight million

[1] Pecqueur, *De la Réforme industrielle* (1832), quoted by H. Bourgin in *RSoc.*, xlv. 417.

[2] 'Quand elle les a *machinisés*' (italics of the original).

[3] Considerant, *Destinée sociale*, i. 261.

[4] Buret, *La Misère des classes laborieuses en Angleterre et en France*.

[5] Sée, op. cit. 91–95.

of them lived on oatmeal, chestnuts, corn mush, and potatoes—bread was a luxury. Twenty-five million scarcely ever tasted wine, and, to protect prices, entire vintages were poured down the gutter. Fourier, who describes this state of affairs, goes on as follows:

The French workers are so destitute that in industrialized provinces like Picardy, between Amiens, Cambrai, and Saint-Quentin, rural workers have no beds in their cabins made of sods. They make a place to lie on with dead leaves which in winter-time turn into worm-filled manure, and so when they get up in the morning fathers and children must pick off worms clinging to their flesh. The food in these shanties is of the same elegance as the furniture. Such is the happy fate of 'la belle France'.[1]

Writing in 1835 of the standard of living of French working-class people, a doctor says: 'Vivre, pour eux, c'est uniquement ne pas mourir.'[2] To earn his meagre pittance, the French workman laboured from thirteen to sixteen hours a day.[3] And it was absolutely necessary for his wife and children to work as well. Some statistics of 1847 show 254,000 women employed to 672,000 men and 131,000 children; a contemporary economist gives the average wages of women workers as 1 franc a day, and 45 to 75 centimes as the wages paid to children.[4]

In the wage-earning class [says a writer of 1833] the children go to work as soon as they have the strength to stand on their feet, or they would be too much of a burden for their parents to support. . . . There are tasks of which children are as capable as men, and their application to such tasks has been welcomed with joy by industrial managers, since it offered them a supply of very cheap labour. The result of the possibility of making

[1] *Le Nouveau Monde industriel*, in *Œuvres*, vi. 30–31.
[2] Quoted by Louis Blanc in *Questions d'aujourd'hui et de demain*, 41.
[3] Sée, op. cit. 94.   [4] Ibid. 91.

money out of the strength of children has been that engineers have sought means of utilizing them on a wider scale. Parents have been encouraged to have larger families and have considered them a benefit, for these little unfortunates eat less than they earn. . . . And so in many working-class families fatherhood has become an economic speculation.[1]

It was not till 1841 that a law was passed governing child-labour. The first piece of labour-legislation in French history, it forbade the employment in factories of children under eight; between the ages of eight and twelve, they were permitted to work not more than eight hours a day, and between twelve and sixteen not more than twelve hours a day. But the law was not enforced, and throughout the Monarchy of July the terrible conditions described by the Romantic poets actually existed.

> Où vont tous ces enfants dont pas un seul ne rit?
> Ces doux êtres pensifs que la fièvre maigrit?
> Ces filles de huit ans qu'on voit cheminer seules?
> Ils s'en vont travailler quinze heures sous des meules;
> Ils vont, de l'aube au soir, faire éternellement
> Dans la même prison le même mouvement . . .[2]

The expectation of life, for these children, was one year and a half from the day of their first going to work.[3]

How can anyone [asks Baudelaire], whatever party one may belong to and whatever prejudices one may have been brought up on, fail to be touched at the sight of this sickly multitude breathing the dust of the factories, swallowing cotton-floss, their systems saturated with white lead, mercury, and all the poisons necessary to the creation of works of art, sleeping amid vermin in quarters where the greatest and simplest of human

[1] Buchez, *Introduction à la science de l'histoire*, 26–27.
[2] This part of Hugo's *Melancholia* was written in 1846. It is contemporaneous with Mrs. Browning's *The Cry of the Children*.
[3] Dolléans, *Histoire du mouvement ouvrier*, i. 21.

virtues nestle by the side of the most hardened vices and the vomit of the penitentiary?[1]

The sense of frustration of which Sainte-Beuve speaks is reflected in the popular drama of the day. In a play of 1832, a workman, pointing to the mockery of democratic principles in such a society, says:

As long as there are rich and poor there is no hope of equality. . . . Look at this factory. Here we are all equal—all as penniless as each other. In the state of civilization we have reached today the strongest smacks down the weakest. That's what I understand by 'equality'.[2]

These are the first stirrings of class-consciousness in modern literature. The workers in heavy industry were really a new class: *l'espèce ouvrière*, a contemporary calls them. The beginnings of the working-class movement go back to 1832–3; and it was from England that the first trade unions spread to the Continent, simultaneously with parliamentary institutions. In 1834 middle-class resistance reached a peak with the deportation of the Dorsetshire workers; the Workhouse Act was passed and in France repressive press-legislation and laws curtailing freedom of association and assembly were enacted the same year. In 1838 the London Working Men's Association launched the appeal for a People's Charter: the Chartist movement, which was the direct outcome of the crisis through which Britain was passing, marks, in the words of its historian, 'the first entry of the masses on the stage of modern history'.[3] In France the pattern for similar associations was set in many cases by the republican Société des Droits de l'Homme, whose membership increased greatly in the

---

[1] *L'Art romantique* (on Pierre Dupont), in *Œuvres* (Pléiade), ii. 408.

[2] Deslandes et Didier, *Étienne et Robert*, drame populaire en un acte représenté sur le Théâtre des Variétés le 11 mai 1832, scène 2.

[3] E. Dolléans, *Le Chartisme* (new edition, Marcel Rivière, 1949).

early years of the July Monarchy as a result of the formation of working-class sections. The left wing of this society
was inspired by the tradition of Babeuf, author, with
Sylvain Maréchal, of the *Manifeste des égaux* of 1796, which
proclaimed that the French Revolution was but the fore-
runner of a greater revolution destined to establish community of wealth and to be the outcome not of co-operative
effort but of the activity of a well-trained and well-
organized minority. The Chartist leader Bronterre O'Brien
drew on this tradition, as did, to a still greater degree,
Karl Marx.

New ideas were meanwhile emerging, products of direct
experience of the rationalization of industry and of the
shocking contrast afforded by the workers' daily lives. And
with them came unfamiliar words: *prolétaire* (borrowed
from Rousseau and the orators of the French Revolution),
capitaliste (first used by Turgot), and, most important of
all, *socialisme*, which enters general circulation in 1834, in
a historic article by Pierre Leroux full of the horror of the
Rue Transnonain massacre.[1] Drawing an impressive parallel with the civil wars of the sixteenth century and the
massacre of Saint Bartholomew's Day, Leroux reflects that
at least, in those days, fanaticism invoked the name of God
and eternal salvation, whereas in 1834 an authority which
is merely the representative of economic class-interests
sends pitiless orders by telegraph to 'transform proletarian
soldiers into executioners of the proletariat'.

France has been called the 'classic land of socialism',[2]
and it was in the writings of Claude Henri de Rouvroy,
Comte de Saint-Simon (1760–1825), that the ideological

[1] Reproduced in my *Socialisme romantique*, 223–38. On early usage
of the term in France and England see R. Picard, 'Sur l'origine des
mots *socialisme* et *socialiste*', *RSoc.*, li (1910), 379–90; E. Halévy, *Histoire du socialisme européen*, 17–18 n.
[2] Gide and Rist, *Histoire des doctrines économiques*.

superstructure of the social movement began to be con-
structed. As one of his biographers says, the story of his
life reads like a film-scenario. A grand-nephew of the Duc
de Saint-Simon who wrote the *Mémoires* of the Court of
Louis XIV, he seems to have determined early to add
further lustre to the family name. At the age of seventeen
he instructed his valet to call him each morning with the
words: 'Levez-vous, Monsieur le comte, vous avez de
grandes choses à faire!'[1] Two years later, as an officer in
the Regiment of Touraine, he took part in the American
War of Independence, distinguished himself at the siege
of Yorktown, was twice wounded, and was decorated with
the Order of Cincinnatus. Thereafter he went to Mexico
where he laid the first plans for a canal at Panama. Returning to France in time to witness the events of the
French Revolution, he enriched himself by land-specula-
tion and devoted himself to the study of philosophy. In
this he was encouraged by a dream he had in prison during
the Terror. Charlemagne, whom he considered one of his
ancestors, appeared to him and said: 'Since the world was
created, no family has enjoyed the honour of producing a
hero and a philosopher of the first rank. My son, your suc-
cesses as a philosopher will equal mine as a statesman.'
The strange thing about this language is that it was actually
prophetic: Napoleon had called Charlemagne *notre auguste
prédécesseur*, but, as M. Thibaudet remarks, 'of these two
Carolingianisms one failed, Napoleon's, and one succeeded,
Saint-Simon's'. In 1801 Saint-Simon married, with the
avowed purpose of entertaining scholars and artists at his
house.[2] The experiment cost him the sum of half a million

---

[1] *Doctrine de Saint-Simon, première année* (Marcel Rivière), 111.

[2] 'J'ai usé du mariage comme d'un moyen pour étudier les savants',
Premier fragment de ma vie. His wife was Mademoiselle de Champ-
grand, later the novelist Madame de Bawr.

francs and was altogether disappointing. He used to com-
plain that the savants who attended his receptions ate too
much and talked too little; often he would find a com-
fortable chair and go to sleep. In 1802, having learned that
Madame de Staël had lost her husband, he divorced his
wife and wrote to the author of *De la littérature considérée
dans ses rapports avec les institutions sociales* proposing
marriage. Meanwhile Saint-Simon had visited England,
also in the interests of science. He regretted to find that
the inhabitants of that country were 'not directing their
scientific efforts to physico-political ends, that they were
not actively concerned with the reorganization of the
political system and had in hand no new essential ideas'.[1]
Saint-Simon's life during the Empire was one of suffering
and privation. For a few months in 1815 he was assistant
librarian at the Arsenal Library, which now houses an
imposing collection of works and autographs of Saint-
Simon and his disciples. He died in 1825. On his deathbed
he is quoted as saying to Olinde Rodrigues, his secretary:
'Souvenez-vous que pour faire de grandes choses, il faut
être passionné.'[2]

Saint-Simon's writings are distinguished by prophetic
acumen rather than scientific precision. His first work appeared in 1802 in collaboration with Augustin Thierry, the
future historian of the Norman Conquest. It was entitled
Lettres d'un habitant de Genève à ses contemporains. This
was followed (1814) by a treatise *De la réorganisation de la
société européenne* containing a scheme for a European
Parliament of Nations,[3] and by a number of works on

[1] *Premier fragment de ma vie.* Quoted by Hugo in his 'Journal d'un
révolutionnaire de 1830', *Littérature et philosophie mêlées* (Hetzel), 159.
[2] *Le Globe*, 30 December 1831.
[3] Rousseau and the Abbé de Saint-Pierre are important forerunners
of Saint-Simon, as are Kant, Condorcet, and William Penn. The earliest French plan of perpetual peace is that of Pierre Dubois (1350).

social and economic questions, chief of which are *Du système industriel* (1821–2), *Catéchisme des Industriels* (1823–4), and *Nouveau Christianisme* (1825). In 1817 with the aid of a subsidy of 10,000 francs a month from the banker Laffitte he published a review, *L'Industrie*. Among his other supporters were the Duke of La Rochefoucauld; Casimir Périer; the Pereire family, founders of a dynasty of bankers; Vital Roux, Governor of the Bank of France; the scientist Cuvier; the liberal economist Jean-Baptiste Say; Lafayette; and the great actor Talma. *L'Industrie* was the first of many Saint-Simonian journals.

In the trend of civilization in the early nineteenth century Saint-Simon saw both a promise and a danger. He apprehended the rise of an economic feudalism in the place of the political, and to forestall it proposed the creation of what he called an 'Industrial State', in which the machinery of government was to be organized on rational lines for the 'exploitation of the globe by the material, intellectual, and moral activity of mankind in association'. With its establishment the class-war would come to an end, and a classless society would ensue. Art, science, and industry were the sources to which Saint-Simon looked for initiative; and in those representing them he proposed to vest the responsibility of management. He was not a democrat. The doctrine of popular sovereignty he rejected as too arbitrary. Only socially useful 'capacities' seemed to him fitted to govern; the mass of men were mere parasites. An aristo-

Victor Considerant, in 1841, proposed an *Unité fédérale des nations*, and specified that to have any chance of success the nations comprising it must be democracies capable of raising, in case of need, an international army: *Bases de la politique positive*, 2nd ed., 215. Another important contribution to peace-literature was made by Proudhon, who declared in 1862: 'Le XXe siècle ouvrira l'ère des fédérations, ou l'humanité recommencera un purgatoire de mille ans.' *Du principe fédératif*, 109.

crat by birth, his main preoccupation in all his works is with the problem of a new managerial oligarchy. The evaluation which he made of 'capacities' will best appear from his famous parable, written and actually published in 1819.

If France were suddenly to lose her 50 leading physicists, her 50 leading chemists, physiologists, mathematicians, poets, painters, sculptors, musicians, her 50 leading mechanics, engineers, architects, doctors, surgeons, pharmacists, her 50 leading bankers, business men, farmers, factory-owners, tanners, dyers, miners, . . . in all, the 3,000 leading scientists, artisans, and artists in the country—the nation would become a body without a soul, and would fall into such a state of inferiority with regard to rival nations that it would take it at least a whole generation to repair such a disaster . . . .

If, on the other hand, France were to lose on the same day Monsieur (the King's brother), My Lords the Duke of Angou-lême, the Duke of Berry, the Duke of Orléans, the Duke of Bourbon, . . . all the great officers of the Crown, all the minis-ters of State, all the cardinals, bishops, marshals, . . . civil ser-vants, and in addition the 10,000 richest landowners of those who live nobly—such an accident would certainly grieve the French people, because they are a kind-hearted people, but the loss of the 30,000 individuals reputed to be the most important in the State could cause them only a sentimental regret, for no political harm could result to the State from such a loss, for the reason that it would be very easy to fill the vacancies: there are a great many Frenchmen capable of exercising the functions of King's brother as well as does Monsieur, or of occupying the position of princes as well as the Dukes of Angoulême, Orléans, and Bourbon. . . . A good many shop-assistants are as capable as our Ministers of State. . . . And as for the 10,000 landowners living nobly, their heirs would need no apprenticeship to do the honours as well as they do.[1]

---

[1] Œuvres choisies, ii. 395 ff. The parable first appeared in Saint-Simon's journal L'Organisateur (not to be confused with the later

Upon his death in 1825 Saint-Simon's followers devoted themselves to the task of publicizing his doctrines in
the journals *Le Producteur* (1825–6), *L'Organisateur* (1829–
31), and *Le Globe* (1831–2), as well as in public lectures held
in 1829 and 1830.[1] Many of them were young engineers
from the École Polytechnique, attracted by his interpretation of the doctrine of Progress. Others were bankers and
business men. Their programme was at first entirely real-
istic, consisting of the following main principles:

1. The creation of a 'World Association';[2]

2. The organization of industry for peaceful production;

3. The production and distribution of wealth in accor-
dance with the principle 'A chacun selon sa capacité, à chaque
capacité selon ses œuvres',[3] i.e. each doing the work for
which he is best qualified, and rewards being according to
service. As a first step, the right of inheritance was to be
abolished and a State Bank was to be made the common
pool of the instruments of production. In return, on the
State would devolve the duty of controlling production[4]
and of instituting a 'new social order' founded not on
birth and fortune but on 'capacity'.

journal of that name) and was reprinted in pamphlet form (November 1819). The author was acquitted of the charge of treason, but the
paper was suppressed.

[1] These lectures were published in 1830, in two volumes entitled
Doctrine de Saint-Simon. Exposition.

[2] ASSOCIATION UNIVERSELLE. *Doctrine* (Rivière), 203 *et passim*. This
is the key-word of the socialism of the Romantic period.

[3] *Doctrine* (Rivière), 117, and motto of *Le Globe*. The difference
between this formula and Saint-Simon's *De chacun selon ses moyens
à chacun selon son besoin* is noteworthy. It was the *Doctrine* of 1830
which introduced the notion of property not as an individual right but
as the ownership of 'instruments of production', and of that ownership as a 'fonction sociale' (*Doctrine*, 257). The Romantic writers in
speaking of the 'fonction du poète', i.e. the poet's responsibilities to
society, borrow both term and concept from Saint-Simonian sociology.

[4] 'Diriger la production, la mettre en harmonie avec la consomma-
tion.' *Doctrine*, 261.

Their views on these subjects were often far in advance of their times, as indeed were those of Saint-Simon himself. Here, for example, is the conception of modern warfare we find in 1817:

Should the Government wish to make war, getting *killers* is not its chief concern: it is to industry that it turns, first to raise money, and then to purchase all the materials it needs, obtaining them from industry with the money it has taken from industry. It is industry that supplies government with guns and rifles and ammunition and uniforms, &c., &c. Today, it is no longer *armies* that constitute the military might of a country, but *industry*. . . . Their merit consists only in consuming the products of *industry*; the army which is best supplied with them always gains the advantage, except in cases of absolute incapacity on the part of its *generals*.[1]

The bankers of the early industrial era who gave material encouragement to Saint-Simon were alive to the menace to their new system of modern warfare brought about by competition for foreign markets, and were anxious to come to rational arrangements calculated to keep the peace. Those who compare Utopian socialism with scientific are apt to forget that the workers of the early days of capitalism were not employed by great impersonal corporations. Their employers were individuals, and treated their employees, as Pecqueur says, with a familiarity, but often also with a respect, born of personal relations.[2] And it seemed not irrational to hope for changes by consent and by persuasion, at a time when industrial relations were still relations between human beings. Pecqueur in fact predicts that 'many rich men will devote their capital to the welfare of their workers by giving them a share in the profits and

---

[1] *Œuvres de Saint-Simon et d'Enfantin*, xix. 148–9. From Saint-Simon's *L'Industrie*. Italics of the original.
[2] *Économie sociale*, i. 271.

taking themselves no other share than the reward of their own labour as managers'. He is not thinking only of the example set by Robert Owen, for he continues:

There is at the present time in Europe a universal acclaim of goodwill in favour of the wage-earning classes. There is general sympathy with their sufferings, recognition of the justice of their demands; a mounting tide of condemnation for the brutal hostilities of which they are the first victims . . . impels the search for a social issue from the industrial impasse in which masters and men find themselves—the desperate competition which depreciates human labour.[1]

The socialism of Marx is the product of a more highly evolved industrial society; that, and not any lack of the Utopian spirit, is primarily what distinguishes it from social Romanticism.

The young organizers who took up Saint-Simon's ideas after his death shared the Romantic belief that rational doctrines need a religious sanction, and they presented their 'new social order' as a 'religion' of which they were themselves the 'disciples' and of which Saint-Simon was the 'Messiah'. Renan, who felt sympathetic to Saint-Simonism in other respects, thought that but for this the doctrine might have become 'the original philosophy of nineteenth-century France'.[2] Be that as it may, in December 1829 under the leadership of one Prosper Enfantin (thereafter known as 'Le Père') a religious hierarchy was ceremoniously set up. Enfantin was a graduate of the École Polytechnique who while in the banking business at St. Petersburg (1821–3) had interested himself in the writings of Adam Smith and Jean-Baptiste Say. Introduced to the ideas of Saint-Simon by Rodrigues, his former teacher at the École Polytechnique, he brought to the movement a force of

[1] Op. cit. ii. 30–31, 111–12.
[2] L'Avenir de la Science (Calmann-Lévy), 104.

character and personal magnetism reminiscent of a Russian mystic.[1] He and Bazard were proclaimed the Fathers of the *Religion Saint-Simonienne*. Bazard, a Republican and one of the leading spirits of the secret *carbonaro* society, represented the more rational element and, to quote one of the disciples, 'while Enfantin, carried away by his temperament, remained in contemplation before the Trinity, Bazard applied himself to the problem of a constitution for the people. He was the organizer; his political sense never wavered.'[2] A violent conflict presently arose between the two leaders. Its direct cause was the issue of feminism. Of this Saint-Simon had said little beyond affirming that there should be equality between the sexes and that women should be permitted to participate in a subscription for a fitting memorial to Newton.[3] But Père Enfantin was intensely interested in the 'rehabilitation of the Flesh'. The term was understood to apply to those material values which Catholicism was accused of having despised, and the Saint-Simonian doctrine was specifically concerned with the expansion of industry and the improvement of the status of workers; but Enfantin went farther, and in the metaphysical urge to commune with the universal animate substance of things demanded a Woman Messiah, to preside over the destinies of the movement in association with himself. Bazard, a middle-aged married man, was not to be convinced. Discussions went on within the group all

[1] M. Viatte has recently established a connexion between the mysticism of Enfantin and the Catholic illuminism of the late Restoration period. Auguste Viatte, *Victor Hugo et les illuminés de son temps* (Montreal, L'Arbre, 1942), 57, 104.

[2] J. Reynaud, 'Bazard', *Encyclopédie Nouvelle* (Gosselin, 1836), ii. 522.

[3] *Lettres d'un habitant de Genève à ses contemporains*, 521. He was also quoted as saying: 'L'individu social, c'est l'homme et la femme' (*Œuvres*, xliv. 399); and this was the basis on which Enfantin founded his doctrine of free divorce and 'religious promiscuity'.

day and all night; some of the disciples would prophesy, in
an ecstatic trance, others were seized with convulsions and
were thought to be full of the Holy Ghost. Eventually
Bazard and many others seceded, but the search for 'La
Mère' went eagerly on.

Meanwhile the doctrine had spread to the provinces and
to distant countries. In 1830–1 groups were organized all
over France and thousands of converts were made. A
special effort was made to interest the working class in
Paris and Lyons. As a result, the Saint-Simonians were
blamed for the riots in the latter city, quite wrongly,
since their propaganda was in fact counter-revolutionary.
In Belgium the chief centres were at Brussels, Liége, and
Louvain; and a paper, *L'Organisateur belge* (1831), was
published. Saint-Simonism was introduced to Germany
by Heine and Lorenz von Stein. The Young German
movement was largely influenced by it. In 1835 Heine
dedicated his *De l'Allemagne* to Enfantin; he described
Saint-Simonism as 'the invisible church which is everywhere and nowhere'.[1] Goethe received the *Globe* regularly,
finding in its pages, as he once said, much to interest him
three times a week; and it is tempting to recognize traces
of Saint-Simonism in the *Second Faust*, especially the
final two acts which celebrate the transformation of the
globe by 'art', or technology.[2] Especially important was
the influence of the doctrine upon German socialism. It
dates from Lorenz von Stein's *Der Sozialismus und Commu-
nismus des heutigen Frankreichs* (1842) and Karl Grün's
Die soziale Bewegung in Frankreich und Belgien (1845).
Though Marx called the Saint-Simonians 'half prophets
and half crooks' he knew their writings more thoroughly
than did these writers. His native town, Trèves, was a

[1] Butler, *The Saint-Simonian Religion in Germany*, 104, 112.
[2] G. Friedmann, '*Faust* et Saint-Simon', *Europe*, xxvi (1948), 13–21.

centre for Saint-Simonian propaganda in 1835; and his father belonged to a group which was dissolved by the police on suspicion of engaging in such activities. Later, at the University of Berlin, he studied under Professor Eduard Gans, who interested him both in Hegelian philosophy and in Saint-Simonian literature. His own thought owes much to Saint-Simonism.[1] The socialization of the means of production; the expropriation of landed property; the abolition of the right of inheritance ('un vestige féodal', says Bazard, 'la propriété *par droit de naissance* et non par droit de capacité');[2] the centralization of credit in the hands of the State by the establishment of a State Bank with an exclusive monopoly: these demands were all made by the Saint-Simonians long before they appeared in the *Communist Manifesto*. By his conception of the class struggle, of the 'exploitation of man by man';[3] and by his interpretation of the process of emergence of governing classes Marx continually recalls Bazard. Like the Saint-Simonians he looked forward to a future society in which class 'antagonisms' shall have given way to the great principle of 'association'.[4] He differed from them in

[1] Andler, *Le Manifeste communiste de Karl Marx et F. Engels*; G. Gurvitch, 'La Sociologie du jeune Marx', *CIS*. iv (1948), 11 ff.

[2] *Doctrine, seconde année* (Paris, 1830), 159.

[3] 'L'exploitation de l'homme par l'homme', a term introduced by the Saint-Simonians, first appears in the *Doctrine, première année* (Rivière, p. 74 *et passim*); the *Producteur* (1825–6) speaks only of the *exploitation du globe terrestre*, as does Saint-Simon himself. An English writer of 1858 finds it necessary to explain the meaning by reference to the French (William Lucas Sargant, *Social Innovators and Their Schemes*, London, Smith Elder [1858], 42–43: chapter on Saint-Simon); in the same chapter he explains the word *prolétaire* 'for the sake of some readers who may have seen this word without clearly apprehending its meaning' (op. cit. 93).

[4] *Manifesto*, § 54. Communist society is, like the *nouvel ordre social* of which the *Doctrine* speaks, to be a progressive, and not a static, society. In the conclusion of his *Misère de la philosophie* Marx writes (in French): 'Ce n'est que dans un ordre de choses où il n'y aura plus

his insistence that its realization could not come till the class war had reached its inevitable consummation in a series of world-shaking disasters. He rejected the Saint-Simonian assumption that an intellectual élite could convince the governing classes against their own interests, and believed in the necessity of the 'violent overthrow of the whole contemporary social order' by the organized proletariat. The Saint-Simonian philosophy of history was evolutionist rather than revolutionary.[1] Based on the dynamism of Progress, it recognized in human experience organic and critical stages, the organic periods being those (such as the Middle Ages) at which social institutions, and, in general, all forms of human activity, answer some well understood and universally accepted social purpose, and the critical periods those during which the absence of such a sense of purpose breaks down the bonds of fellow-feeling and mutual understanding and leads (as in modern times) to the conflict of selfish interests, the cut-throat competition and virtual civil war which then pass for civilization.[2] The *Doctrine* of 1830 opens with a picture of contemporary society split into two warring camps: reaction and revolution; and of its institutions in ruins 'because they have ceased to be in harmony with the exigencies of a new society'.[3] This feeling that institutions must be 'in harmony with the times' is fundamentally romantic. Before emerging in the science of sociology it appears in Stendhal's rejection of Racinian tragedy and demand for a literature to interest the argumentative young men of 1823. What an

de classes et d'antagonisme de classes que les évolutions sociales cesseront d'être des révolutions politiques.'

[1] 'C'est une *évolution* qu'elle vient prédire et accomplir.' *Doctrine* (Rivière), 279.

[2] 'Un vaste état de guerre systématisé.' Ibid. 211; also 127, 195–6, 267.

[3] Ibid., 121–3.

important part was played by the evolutionist philosophy of history in the development of economic and political thought is beginning to be realized.[1] In England, Carlyle, initiated into it in 1830 by Gustave d'Eichthal, one of Saint-Simon's most enthusiastic disciples, was greatly attracted. In *Sartor Resartus* he quotes 'that strange aphorism of Saint-Simon's concerning which and whom so much were to be said',

The golden age which a blind tradition has hitherto laid in the past is not behind us but before us. It lies in the perfecting of the social order.[2]

Carlyle translated Saint-Simon's *Nouveau Christianisme*, and in his *Chartism* and *Past and Present* the Saint-Simonian influence is marked. John Stuart Mill was a personal friend of d'Eichthal, with whom he corresponded for many years. He became acquainted with the Saint-Simonian school in 1829–30, and was 'greatly struck', he says, 'with the connected view which they for the first time presented to me of the natural order of human progress, and especially with their division of all history into organic periods and critical periods'.[3] Of their publications one left a decisive impression on him. This was one of the early writings of Auguste Comte, entitled *Plan des travaux scientifiques nécessaires pour réorganiser la société* and published in 1822 in the third *cahier* of Saint-Simon's *Catéchisme des Industriels*, the author's name being followed by the words *élève de Saint-Simon*. Mill's correspondence with d'Eichthal shows that he followed the fortunes of the

---

[1] Grossman, 'The Evolutionist Revolt against Classical Economics.' *JPE*. li (1943), 381–96.

[2] *Sartor Resartus* (Chapman & Hall, 1872), 163–4. The text is from *De la réorganisation de la société européenne*, and was used as a motto by *Le Producteur*. *Sartor Resartus* was written in 1831.

[3] *Autobiography* (London, 1873), 163.

Saint-Simonians for many years.[1] D'Eichthal introduced him in 1830 to Bazard and Enfantin. He too received the *Globe*, and testifies in a letter of November 1831 to d'Eichthal that he never read an article in it that did not have its effect.[2] He evidently read the *Doctrine de Saint-Simon*,[3] and recognizes in his *Autobiography* that he owed to it an early realization of the inadequacy of political liberalism:

Their criticisms of the common doctrines of Liberalism seemed to me full of important truth; and it was partly by their writings that my eyes were opened to the very limited and temporary value of the old political economy which assumes private property and inheritance as indefeasible facts and freedom of production and exchange as the *dernier mot* of social improvement. The scheme gradually unfolded by the Saint-Simonians, under which the labour and capital of society would be managed for the general account of the community, every individual being required to take a share of labour, either as thinker, teacher, artist, or producer, all being classed according to their capacity and remunerated according to their work, appeared to me a far superior description of Socialism to Owen's. . . . I honoured them most of all for what they have been most cried down for—the boldness and freedom from prejudice with which they treated the subject of family, the most important of any, and needing more fundamental alterations than remain to be made in any other great social institution, but on which scarcely any reformer has the courage to touch. In proclaiming the perfect equality of men and women, and an entirely new order of things in regard to their relations with one another, the Saint-Simonians, in common with Owen and Fourier, have entitled themselves to the grateful remembrance of future generations.[4]

[1] E. d'Eichthal, *John Stuart Mill. Correspondance inédite avec Gustave d'Eichthal* (Paris, Alcan, 1898).

[2] *Letters*, ed. by Hugh Elliot (Longmans, 1910), i. 21.

[3] 'As long as their public teachings and proselytism continued, I read nearly everything they wrote.' *Autobiography*, 166.

[4] Ibid. 166–8.

Among the other benefits which he personally derived from Saint-Simonian literature Mill enumerates the 'clearer conception' he obtained of 'the peculiarities of an era of transition in opinion'.

That all questions of political institutions are relative, not absolute, and that different stages of human progress not only *will* have, but *ought* to have, different institutions: that government is always in the hands, or passing into the hands, of whatever is the strongest power in society, and that what this power is does not depend on institutions, but institutions on it: that any general theory or philosophy of politics supposes a previous theory of human progress, and that this is the same thing with a philosophy of history,[1]

—such, according to Mill, were some of the *idées-forces* he derived from the French ideologies of his time and from reading Coleridge, Carlyle, and Goethe. A series of articles entitled 'The Spirit of the Age' and reflecting his new opinions appeared in the *Examiner* early in 1831 and led to his personal acquaintance with Carlyle. In 1832 Mill joined Carlyle in welcoming to England a Saint-Simonian mission headed by d'Eichthal and Charles Duveyrier.[2] The mission visited a number of industrial centres and engaged in propaganda in favour of the union of the working classes and of the industrial leaders of France and England. It returned to France with the report that the England of 1832 (the year of the Reform Bill) was on the threshold of a social revolution, that the working class was organizing, and looking for leaders, and that the British

[1] Op. cit. 165, 162.
[2] Duveyrier's drama in praise of the engineer, *L'Ingénieur ou la mine de charbon* (1836), is typical of the movement. Vigny went to see it at the Porte Saint-Martin and exercised his ingenuity discovering in it a 'hidden meaning'. *Journal d'un poète* (Scholartis Press), 103–4. An earlier play of Duveyrier's, *Le Monomane*, produced in 1835, is a possible source of Brieux's *La Robe rouge*.

would be 'the first nation of the new order'.[1] But its actual results were rather disappointing, for reasons which appear in one of Mill's letters:

In England the idea of any reform beginning in people's *minds*, through preaching to them a general doctrine, is a notion that would never enter anyone's head. . . . The British people usually distrust the most obvious truths if the person who sets them forth can be suspected of having general ideas. To influence people in this country you must first carefully hide the fact that you possess a system or organized set of opinions; you must teach isolated facts, and try to educate people to think by dealing with simple, practical questions. Once you are known and respected as one who has a good knowledge of facts and a shrewd appreciation of detail, you may venture some original views; but even then you must be very prudent and circumspect.[2]

It was at this period that the true disciples of Saint-Simon according to Enfantin were making an experiment in communal living. Some forty disciples set up a community at Ménilmontant, 'dans la maison du Père', where they tilled the soil to the singing of hymns, and with much ceremonial prepared themselves for the coming of La Mère. Bearded and long-haired like the bohemian Jeunes-France, they adopted a peculiar uniform, including a vest buttoned at the back to remind them that the individual is helpless without the co-operation of his fellow men. Enfantin himself wore a red toque rather like a Turkish fez, a tight-fitting blue coat, and white trousers; across his chest he wore a ribbon with the words LE PÈRE. The disciples 'abolished domesticity' and were romantically called to their meals by the sound of the horn, until in August 1832 they were summoned to appear in court on

[1] D'Allemagne, *Les Saint-Simoniens*, 156.
[2] E. d' Eichthal, *John Stuart Mill. Correspondance inédite avec G. d'Eichthal*, 127.

the charge of being an illegal society and of 'outraging public morals'. The leaders were sent to jail for a year, and the co-operative commonwealth came to an end.

After Enfantin's release a mission left for the East in quest of the Femme Messie. They were known as the 'Compagnons de la Femme' and considered themselves as modern crusaders. They were welcomed at Beyrouth by Lady Hester Stanhope, whom the Arabs called Queen of Jerusalem. She was sixty years of age, and was waiting for the advent of a male Messiah. For many years she had been prophesying that a Frenchman would establish a new universal religion: Lamartine, who made a trip to the East the same year, had recently visited her and had been told that he was 'un de ces hommes que j'attendais, que la Providence m'envoie'.[1] Presently the Crusaders had a revelation: the Mère was in India. Enfantin joined them in Egypt, and there after a vain effort to persuade the Egyptian authorities to undertake a canal at Suez they were commissioned to construct a Nile Dam. Construction work on this project, begun on 12 May 1834, continued till 1838 when an outbreak of plague, which carried off many members of the group, caused it to be abandoned. The survivors returned to live in a despised society in which nearly all of them achieved success and fame. They became in fact what Carlyle was the first to call Captains of Industry. Père Enfantin himself, after spending some time in Algeria (1840–1), emerged a Director of the P.L.M. railway, and a person who saw this mystical figure in 1846 describes him as 'a gentleman interested in railways, and looking quite the part'. The creation of the French transport system was the work of these Romantic poly-technicians, carried out in the face of government

[1] On Lady Stanhope see Lytton Strachey's essay in *Books and Characters* (New York, 1922), 297–307.

opposition. Local services (Lyons–Saint-Étienne 1832, Paris–Versailles 1836–9, Paris–Saint-Germain 1837, &c.) they merged into great national arteries, and went on to build railways in Spain, Russia, Austria-Hungary, and Switzerland. The project of engineering the Suez Canal was first conceived by a Saint-Simonian, Fournel. The plans were communicated by Enfantin to Ferdinand de Lesseps who was Vice-consul in Egypt at the time of the arrival of the Compagnons de la Femme; and de Lesseps it was who obtained the concession (1854), ignoring completely Enfantin and the 'Société d'études pour le canal de Suez' formed in 1846. Other Saint-Simonians played a large part in equipping the capitalist system with its indispensable banking and credit institutions. The Crédit Foncier and Crédit Mobilier were both founded by the Pereire brothers, who also assisted in the creation of the Comptoir d'Escompte. Their influence was felt in Germany, where the bankers Oppenheimer and Mevissen, associated with the Saint-Simonians, founded the Darmstädter Bank on the lines of the Crédit Mobilier.

Nor did the primitive Saint-Simonian ideology disappear with the disintegration of the central organization. Many Saint-Simonian ideas survive today, and some have been transformed, or are in process of being transformed, into institutions. The idea of international intellectual co-operation sponsored by the United Nations, to give one example, is characteristically Saint-Simonian. In 1803 Saint-Simon proposed a memorial to Newton, to be erected by international subscription; it was to be situated on international territory and was to comprise a library, a school, and model laboratories. The whole institution was to be controlled by a Council of Scholars who would be guaranteed freedom to work in peace and would upon occasion offer advice to the various national governments. It should be

019905

noted that Saint-Simon always insisted upon the need to organize the conditions of intellectual life with the same care and efficiency as those surrounding material life. He emphasized the importance to the State of discovering intellectual ability and fostering it wherever found. He demanded an open road to educational privileges for young men of talent irrespective of means, 'l'équitable égalité du point de départ', as he described it, or, as we say, equality of opportunity. As a means to this end his followers proposed the creation of a Crédit Intellectuel by the side of the other credit institutions they were engaged in establishing. Their view that intellectual capacity constitutes socially desirable security for the investment of funds failed to convince their contemporaries, but the idea was not wholly lost,[1] and is even now receiving belated recognition with the creation of national scholarship funds.

It is a striking paradox that whereas Marxism, the socialism of a university man, makes its appeal to the working class, Saint-Simonism which is an engineer's or business man's socialism addresses itself pre-eminently to intellectuals and concerns itself with their function in society. Let us recall in this connexion that Saint-Simon himself considered the intelligentsia the representatives in modern society of the spiritual authority. His followers made a special effort to enlist the sympathies of contemporary writers. The journal *Le Producteur* announces it as its purpose to 'foster the union of scientists, industrialists, and artists, as the only means of rescuing society from its present state of crisis'.[2] It attaches the greatest importance to literature, and calls it 'the living expression of the forms and needs of society' and 'a powerful lever for the develop-

---

[1] It was revived in 1921 and made the subject of a special number of a neo-Saint-Simonian journal, *Le Producteur*, started in 1920.

[2] Prospectus, 4.

ment of moral energies'.[1] The liberal economists, it complains, were too exclusively concerned with the problems of material production, and underestimated the importance of *moral* or *intellectual production*.[2] Society as a whole is 'becoming more and more positive', and the arts have everything to lose if they neglect their opportunity to 'serve the common cause by propagating generous ideas' and thus advancing 'the general movement of the human intelligence'.[3] Some *Philosophical Considerations on Literature* (1825) by A. Cerclet study the 'social function' which literature has to perform.[4] And in *Reflections on Literature and the Fine Arts*, Buchez declares in 1826: 'Literature and the fine arts are not the works of idleness and dissipation; they are the creations of passionate sentiments, that is to say, of all that is least individualistic in man.' A little farther, he goes on to define these as 'le sentiment du collectisme', 'the sense of social purpose which becomes the motive of the artist's every act and the source of all his passionate inspirations.'[5] Of all forms of literature, it was the drama in which the Saint-Simonians were most interested. Devoting a series of articles to 'L'Art théâtral considéré dans ses moyens d'utilité publique', Buchez proclaims in 1832: 'Art today must have social usefulness. It must appeal to the people. The theatre in particular must have this double purpose; for, next to the public platform and the press, society has no more powerful medium of education.'[6]

The writers of the Romantic school in France were quick to detect the prophetic note in the doctrines of Saint-Simon and of his disciples; indeed, the measure of

[1] Prospectus, 5.
[2] Ibid. 3. Italics of the original.
[3] Ibid. 13–14.
[4] Vol. i, p. 59.
[5] *Le Producteur*, iv. 190–4.
[6] *L'Européen*, 7 April 1832.

success which has attended those doctrines is largely owing
to the diffusion they received in the novels of Victor Hugo
and George Sand, and in the works of Vigny. Human
beings—the Saint-Simonians were right—will always be
more amenable to reasoning when it is diluted with
sentiment; and the arguments of the early socialists might
have been relatively futile without the appeal which the
poet, the dramatist, and the novelist were able to make. To
the credit of the Romantic movement should be laid the
enormous contribution which it made to the sense of
social solidarity. This has been little recognized except by
sociologists and historians. M. Charléty points to the influence of Saint-Simonism upon the sacerdotal conception
of art held by the Romantic writers, especially Hugo, and
shows how the view of literature as a *function* led to the
creation of the social novel and thesis play.[1] M. Louis
Maigron in his account of the influence of Romanticism
upon French manners shows that though many young
women like Madame Bovary, already somewhat unbal-
anced, were completely demoralized as a result of reading
George Sand or Byron, the Romantic movement 'instilled
into the public mind respect for the personality; and
developed, more than any other literary doctrine, the sense
of pity for the weak and the disinherited'.[2] The conventional picture of the typical Romantic as a 'jeune homme
désespéré qui pleure sur un roc solitaire'[3] has nothing in
common with Hugo's view of the movement. He saw in it
a 'force of civilization' stemming from the revolutionary
tradition,[4] and there is much to support his point of view,

---

[1] *Histoire du Saint-Simonisme*, 357–8.

[2] *Le Romantisme et les mœurs, essai d'étude historique et sociale
d'après des documents inédits* (Paris, Champion, 1910), 385–9.

[3] Bouglé in *Le Romantisme et les lettres*, 267–81.

[4] *William Shakespeare* (Ollendorff), 401. All references to Hugo
apply to this edition, unless otherwise stated. Cf. 'Les poètes du

especially in the Romantic literature of France. English literature exhibits the same trend in the novels of Charles Dickens, George Eliot, Charles Kingsley, Mrs. Gaskell, and Harriet Beecher Stowe,[1] the poems of Mrs. Browning and Thomas Hood, and the essays of Carlyle and Ruskin. In Russia, the home of the modern social novel and drama, the movement begins with Dostoievsky and Turgenev, whose first works appeared in 1844-7. In France some Romantic writers engaged in the social struggle on the side of the proletariat as early as 1830.

The date of this important departure is set not by the Revolution of July but by the fact that the journal *Le Globe*, hitherto a leading literary organ, was sold to the Saint-Simonians in October of that year.

The same year, the preface of *Hernani* appeared with the historic slogan 'la liberté dans l'art, *la liberté dans la société*', and spoke in ringing terms of a literature to interest the people. *Le Dernier Jour d'un condamné* (1832) salutes the Revolution of July and speaks of the society of the Restoration as 'l'édifice social du passé'. It was followed by a series of prose dramas written for propaganda purposes. In the preface of one of these, *Lucrèce Borgia*, we read:

Many social questions are involved in literary questions, and every literary work is an act. . . . The theatre today has an enormous importance, one which tends to increase with the progress of civilization itself. The theatre is a rostrum. The theatre is a pulpit. The theatre speaks powerfully and loud. . . . The author of this drama is aware that the drama, without transgressing the impartial limits of art, has a national mission, a social mission, a human mission.

dix-neuvième siècle . . . sont les fils de la Révolution Française.' *Post-scriptum de ma vie. Philosophie*, ii. 473.

[1] *Oliver Twist* appeared in 1838, *Uncle Tom's Cabin* in 1852. See Cazamian, *Le Roman social en Angleterre, 1830-1850* (Société nouvelle de librairie et d'édition, 1904).

The outlines of *Les Misérables* begin to appear at the same period. In *Claude Gueux* (1834) Hugo took up his pen to defend an unemployed workman who had been imprisoned for stealing a loaf of bread to give to his starving wife and children, and who while in prison had committed murder. Addressing the Members of Parliament, he wrote:

You are quarrelling about the question whether the buttons of the national guard should be white or yellow. . . . Gentlemen, consider this. The majority of the people are suffering. . . .The people are hungry. The people are cold. Poverty is driving them to crime or vice. . . . You have too many convicts, too many prostitutes.

What do these two ulcers prove, if not that the body social suffers from impurities in the blood-stream?

Hugo was too late to save the life of Claude Gueux. But the 'substitution of social questions for political questions' demanded in the Avant-propos to *Littérature et philosophie mêlées* (1834) clearly indicates the important change which had taken place in his own mind since he wrote the Royalist *Odes*. He committed himself henceforth to the cause of the masses, conscientiously exercising a 'function' which he already regarded as *presque un sacerdoce*.[1]

Though retaining traces of the technocratic outlook of the Saint-Simonians, *Ruy Blas* (1838) is devoted to that mission, and contrasts with Vigny's *Chatterton*, written on a similar theme, in this respect, that the love of the Queen for a lackey denotes a sort of royal sanction or *pitié suprême* for the democratic cause. Ruy Blas's address to the ministers, in which a man of the people denounces the stigmas of a decadent society and the selfishness and corruption of the governing class, is too well known to need quoting. Victor Hugo himself, some years later, paid a visit to the great manufacturing centre of Lille, and

[1] *Littérature et philosophie mêlées*, 6, 15.

wrote a record of actual working-class living-conditions
whose social realism can be demonstrated: for power of
indignation, it matches the great soliloquy of the Romantic
drama. At Lille in those days, and at Liverpool and
Manchester too, textile workers lived in crowded attics or
underground cellars rented sometimes at 4 to 6 shillings
a week, and affording not more than eight square yards
of living-space a head.

> Un jour je descendis dans les caves de Lille;
>   Je vis ce morne enfer.
> Des fantômes sont là sous terre dans des chambres,
> Blêmes, courbés, ployés; le rachis tord leurs membres
>   Dans son poignet de fer . . .
>
> Là dort le désespoir sur son haillon sordide;
> Là l'avril de la vie, ailleurs tiède et splendide,
>   Ressemble au noir hiver . . .
> Là, quand j'entrai, farouche, aux méduses pareille,
> Une petite fille à figure de vieille
>   Me dit: j'ai dix-huit ans!
> Caves de Lille, on meurt sous vos plafonds de pierre!

That men were dying while industry was thriving is
literally true. Here is a letter written by a workman of
Lille at the same period:

I am a textile-worker [he says] earning 2 francs a day, the
maximum wage for a weaver. My wife is a lace-worker,
working at home, and earning 15 centimes a day. We have
four children, the eldest is 10.

—We consume 23 kilos of dark bread a week at 22
centimes . . . . 5 fr. 18
—Meat is too dear, we can only afford offal, three
times a week at 25 centimes. . . . · 75
—Butter, for myself only, ½ lb. a week . . · 50
—My wife and children eat treacle and fruit with
their bread . . . . . . · 80

—Potatoes and beans	.	.	.	.	.	1 fr. 00
—Milk (half a pint a day)	.	.	.	.	.	45
—Rent of a cellar 9 feet under ground	.	.	.	1	50
—Coal	.	.	.	.	.	.	.	1	35
—Soap, light	.	.	.	.	.	.	1	10

Total, per week, 12 fr. 63

We receive from the welfare agency six pounds of dark bread every other week. My eldest daughter spends her holidays with the sisters of charity, and they give her sometimes a hand-kerchief, sometimes a piece of underwear. The three little ones draw every year at Christmas a flannel dress, a shirt, or some-times stockings, from the infants' school. But for all this kindliness and in spite of all our labour, we are living like beggars.[1]

> Caves de Lille, on meurt sous vos plafonds de pierre!
> J'ai vu, vu de mes yeux pleurant sous ma paupière
>   Râler l'aïeul flétri,
> La fille aux yeux hagards de ses cheveux vêtue,
> Et l'enfant spectre au sein de la mère statue! . . .

Hugo was accompanied on his visit to Lille by the statis-tician and economist Adolphe Blanqui; and Blanqui's prosaic description of the working-class quarter blessed with the name of 'Saint-Sauveur' guarantees the humble realities commemorated here in Renaissance stanzas:

It is a series of blocks of dwellings separated by dark, nar-row lanes and leading to tiny back-yards known as *courettes*, used both for drains and to deposit garbage. At all seasons there is a dampness about the place. The windows of the dwel-lings and doors of the cellars open out on these pestilent passages, at the end of which an iron railing stretched over a cesspool serves as a public latrine by day and night. . . . As you enter the

[1] A. M. Gossez, *Mémoires de l'ouvrier François Leblanc*, quoted by A. Pinton in *1848: le Livre du Centenaire* (Éditions Atlas, 1948), 159–60.

courettes a strange population of faded, hunchbacked, and mis-
shapen children, looking pale and grubby, clusters round
the visitors, begging for charity. Most of these unfortunates
are almost naked, and the best provided are covered with
rags. But at least these urchins are able to come out into the
open air, and you must go down into the depths of the cellars
if you want to appreciate the sufferings of those whom age or the
rigour of the season prevent from coming out. Most often they
are all lying there on the bare ground, on the debris of straw,
colza, dried potato-peelings, or sand—anything that may have
been painstakingly gathered together in the course of the day's
work. The pit where they vegetate is entirely bare of furniture;
only to the most fortunate is it given to possess a stove, a chair,
and a few kitchen utensils. One old woman, pointing to a
neighbour stretched out on the damp cellar floor, remarked to
us: 'I am not rich either, but thank God I do have my bit of
straw!'—Over three thousand of our fellow citizens [Blanqui
goes on] are leading this frightful existence in the cellars of
Lille.[1]

Where, the poet asks, shall you find a Dante to describe
this Inferno? And then, having turned from the victims
to the exploiters living joyous lives:

> Ah! quelqu'un parlera. La muse, c'est l'histoire.
> Quelqu'un élèvera la voix dans la nuit noire . . .
> Quelqu'un te vengera, pauvre France abattue,
> Ma mère, et l'on verra la parole qui tue
>   Sortir des cieux profonds!
>
> Ces gueux, pires brigands que ceux des vieilles races,
> Rongeant le pauvre peuple avec leurs dents voraces,
>   Sans pitié, sans merci,
> Vils, n'ayant pas de cœur, mais ayant deux visages,
> Disent: Bah! le poète! Il est dans les nuages!
>   Soit. Le tonnerre aussi.[2]

[1] *Les Classes ouvrières en France en 1848*, i. 98–9.
[2] 'Joyeuse vie', *Les Châtiments* (Hetzel), 94–100.

It was during the Second Republic that Hugo first actually proclaimed himself a socialist; previous to then, the term had been used with specific reference to the doctrines of the Saint-Simonians, of Fourier, and Robert Owen and their disciples. The poet's speeches as a member of the republican assemblies are devoted to the interests of 'la classe nombreuse et laborieuse qui fait la base même de la société'.[1] Of his poems 'Melancholia'[2] and 'Les Pauvres Gens',[3] of his prose writings Les Misérables and Quatre-vingt-treize best illustrate his social thought. The spirit which animates them is essentially the spirit of 1848, for in Hugo's eyes as in Pierre Leroux's 'république et socialisme, c'est un'.[4] On the fifth anniversary of the Revolution of February, Hugo (then living in exile) acclaimed in these terms the revolution of the future:

May the date to come be splendid! May the next revolution be invincible! May it found the United States of Europe!

May it, like February, redeem and place upon its altar the sublime tripod Liberty–Equality–Fraternity! But on that tripod may it kindle so as to enlighten the whole earth the great flame of Humanity![5]

No writer of the century rendered greater service than did Hugo to the cause of social justice. No one in any country strove with greater political independence and personal disinterestedness to create a consciousness of human solidarity. As his biographer says, 'he was under all forms of government the advocate of all the disinherited, all the unfortunate, all the oppressed, nations or individuals; a boundless pity was the unfailing impetus of the social reforms he proposed or supported'.[6] Time after

---

[1] Actes et Paroles, i. 111–12.
[2] Contemplations, III. ii.   [3] Légende des Siècles, LII.
[4] Actes et Paroles, ii (Hetzel), 469.   [5] Op. cit. ii. 139.
[6] Paul Berret, Victor Hugo (Garnier, 1927), 423.

time, in the case of the assassin Barbès whose pardon he secured in 1839 from Louis-Philippe; in the Tapner case in Guernsey; in the case of John Brown on whose behalf he appealed to the United States Government: in these and in many others, he put into practice his noble ideal 'Servir la cause humaine'.[1] Nor should it be forgotten that the words of a Hugo are acts. There can be no doubt that such works as *Les Misérables* and 'Les Pauvres Gens' have had greater effect in arousing the public conscience than all the forty-seven volumes of the *Works* of Saint-Simon and his disciples put together. Bishop Myriel's words to the convict Jean Valjean have a simple eloquence that speaks to the hearts and to the imaginations of all readers.

The Bishop, sitting beside him, gently touched his hand. 'You need not have told me who you were', he said. 'This is not my house, it is the house of Jesus Christ. That door does not ask of him who comes in if he has a name, but only if he has a sorrow. You suffer; you are hungry and thirsty. So you are welcome. And do not thank me, do not say that I am receiving you into my home. No one is at home here, except those who need a place of refuge. I say it to you who pass by: this is your home, more than it is mine. Everything here is yours. What need have I of knowing your name? Besides, before you told it, you had a name I knew.'

The man stared in amazement. 'Is it true? You knew my name?'

'Yes', replied the Bishop. 'You are my brother.'

It was long the fashion to disparage Hugo's novels, but we realize today what a powerful influence they have been in diffusing those democratic principles which in his eyes were the essence of socialism. Tolstoy considered *Les Misérables* the finest work of art of the nineteenth century, and it has been shown how much indebted he was to Hugo

[1] *Contemplations*, v. iii.

when he wrote *Resurrection*.[1] As M. Le Breton says, to write a book like *Les Misérables* requires not only much knowledge but a generous fund of kindness and humanity. Those are the great qualities which Hugo brought to what he called his 'mission'. 'The judge speaks in the name of Justice. The priest' (and, we may read, 'the poet') 'speaks in the name of Pity, which is none other than a higher Justice.'[2] It is his social pity which confers upon so much that Hugo wrote an evangelical tenderness.

> Venez à moi, vous tous qui tremblez, qui souffrez,
> Qui râlez, qui rampez, qui saignez, qui pleurez,
> Les damnés, les vaincus, les gueux, les incurables,
> Venez, venez, venez, venez, ô misérables! . . .[3]

Les Misérables was the culmination of a massive literature of social novels and dramas which flourished between 1830 and 1848. The names of Hugo's predecessors are today justly forgotten, though Eugène Sue, author of *Les Mystères de Paris* (1840), in which the Saint-Simonian influence is very marked, still appeals, with singular propriety, to clients of railway news-stands. The works of George Sand represent the movement quite adequately. A hundred years ago the appearance of a new novel by George Sand was an event hailed not in France only but all over Europe. Today, the socialist novels for which she was notorious are neglected equally with the pastoral idylls *La Mare au Diable*, *François le Champi*, and *La Petite Fadette*, which found so many readers before 1914. But George Sand's life and personality still interest us. Characteristic products of the age, they are the best possible illustration of Saint-Simon's maxim 'Pour faire de grandes choses il faut être passionné'.

[1] André le Breton, 'La Pitié sociale dans le roman', *RDM*, lxxii (1902), 889–915.
[2] *Les Misérables*, I. i. 10 (*Roman*, iii. 45).   [3] *Le Pape*, 131.

In the life of George Sand 1835 was a decisive year. She was then living in Paris, her Venetian adventure with Alfred de Musset being just over. Her feminine genius was exceptionally receptive to personal influences. In April 1835 a radical lawyer, Michel de Bourges, attracted wide attention by his brilliant defence of the leaders in the Lyons riots of the previous year. George Sand fell in love with him, and with republicanism. The same year she made the friendship of Franz Liszt. Liszt it was who interested her in Saint-Simonism;[1] and we find the Paris 'family' sending her as a gift for the new year a hat, a pair of trousers, a vest (*anglice*, waistcoat), a collar and cuffs, flowers, earrings, slippers, fifty-one other articles which cluttered up her apartment, and a thermometer.[2] Addressed 'au génie de la femme qui mettait si vivement en lumière, dans ses œuvres, les plaies sociales dont (*sic*) le sexe le plus faible et la classe la plus nombreuse et la plus pauvre ont à lutter', this tribute was accompanied by an invitation to become the Woman Messiah. While the invitation was not accepted, George Sand's works do bear testimony to her reading of Saint-Simonian literature. The *Réflexions sur Jean-Jacques Rousseau*, for example, contain an interesting version of the Saint-Simonian concept of the artist, and in *Horace* (1842) there is even an attractive picture of the 'femme forte'.

Liszt also, in 1835, introduced George Sand to Lamennais, whom she 'revered as a saint'. This Breton priest, who had read Rousseau at the age of ten and was even then so

---

[1] Liszt used to play at the receptions of the Saint-Simonians in Paris. He composed for the piano a piece entitled *Lyon*, having for its epigraph the slogan of the silk-workers, 'Vivre en travaillant ou mourir en combattant.' He gave a concert for their benefit at Lyons in 1837.

[2] Karénine, *George Sand*, ii. 180, quoting Maxime du Camp's *Mémoires littéraires*. From 1851 to 1858 the *Revue de Paris*, directed by Maxime du Camp, was practically a Saint-Simonian journal.

restless that his school teacher had to anchor him to his seat with a heavy weight, had just published his *Paroles d'un croyant*, which ran to over a hundred editions and was translated into almost every language spoken in Europe. It came out at Renduel's on 3 May 1834, a few weeks before *Chatterton* was begun. An orthodox churchman and convinced royalist in his famous *Essai sur l'indifférence* of 1817–23, Lamennais in his new book appeared as the 'prophet of democracy and of the new age'.[1] Laski has called it 'a lyrical version of the *Communist Manifesto*'.[2] To its author came words of appreciation and encouragement from as far as Canada, while in France Leroux hailed the *Paroles d'un croyant* as 'la Marseillaise du Christianisme'.[3] Describing the state of France in 1835, Lamennais writes to a friend:

Do you not think that there is something strange and even frightening in the contrast between this frivolity and the tremendous revolution which is going on at the heart of human society? While the upper classes, softened by pleasure and luxury, are intoxicated with their *fandango* (the latest dance step), everywhere in the distance a dull rumbling announces the Pyrrhic victory of the peoples. I fail to understand how so many men lacking neither wit nor sense should persist in thinking that the movement is only on the surface, and that it will be appeased without any other result than slight changes in social forms. This movement, believe me, goes to the very depths of humanity, and nothing will appease it till it has produced a new world.[4]

Condemned by a Papal encyclical of 25 June 1835 for his heretical *Paroles*, Lamennais did not cease to exercise a function of spiritual leadership, and his *Affaires de Rome*

[1] Victor Giraud, *La Vie tragique de Lamennais* (Paris, 1933), 115.
[2] H. J. Laski, *Authority in the Modern State* (Oxford, 1919), 255.
[3] Preface to vol. 60 of the *Revue Encyclopédique* (1834).
[4] Letter to Coriolis, quoted by Giraud, op. cit. 157.

(1836), an account of his duel with the Papacy, *Le Livre du peuple* (1837), which revealed him as a great educator of democracy, *De l'esclavage moderne* (1839), a violent denunciation of the wage-system, and *Le Pays et le Gouvernement* (1840), with its warning to conservatives: 'If you reject peaceful reform you will have reform by violence: take your choice', express a spirit epitomized in his own words: 'complete, disinterested devotion to the common cause, and a deep sense of justice cherished for its own sake'.[1] Encouraged by his fearless example, the Romantic writers of the eighteen-thirties broke with orthodoxy and reaction. It is no mere coincidence that the date of publication of the *Paroles d'un croyant* is also that at which the works of Lamartine and Victor Hugo were placed on the Papal Index.[2]

Another religious thinker whom George Sand met in 1835 was Pierre Simon Ballanche, author of the *Essais de palingénésie sociale* (1827–9), *Vision d'Hébal* (1831), and *La Ville des Expiations* (1832), and friend of Chateaubriand and Madame Récamier. What distinguishes Ballanche from other humanitarians of the period is his belief in original sin. Sainte-Beuve testifies to the important effect which his writings had towards 1829 in determining the trend of the Saint-Simonian school to mysticism.[3] He

---

[1] *De l'esclavage moderne*, Marescq 1851, p. 105.

[2] C. Maréchal, *Lamennais, essai d'un système de philosophie catholique* (Champion, 1925). First edition, 1906. Maréchal, *Lamennais et Victor Hugo* (Savaète, 1906), *Lamennais et Lamartine* (Bloud, 1907), *La Jeunesse de Lamennais* (Paris, 1913); F. Duine, *Lamennais, sa vie, ses idées, ses ouvrages* (Paris, 1922), *Bibliographie de Lamennais* (Paris, 1922); A. Viatte, *Le Catholicisme chez les romantiques* (Boccard, 1922), chap. iv; P. Vulliaud, *Les Paroles d'un croyant* (Malfère, 1928); J. Poisson, *Le Romantisme social de Lamennais* (Vrin, 1931); H. J. Laski, *Authority in the Modern State*, 189–280; L. de Villefosse, *Lamennais, ou l'occasion manquée* (Vigneau, 1945).

[3] *Portraits contemporains*, ii. 43.

has also important but inadequately recognized literary affinities, with Balzac and Baudelaire.[1]

Many social doctrines, representing many shades of philosophical and religious thought, flourished side by side in the France of 1835. In her own perplexities the author of *Lélia* turned to Sainte-Beuve, and asked him to aid her in her quest of 'religious and social truth one and the same',[2] i.e. of a doctrine which would enable her to reconcile the religious spirit of Ballanche and of Lamennais with the republicanism of Michel de Bourges and with the social idealism of the Saint-Simonians. Sainte-Beuve thought of a friend and collaborator of the days when he wrote for the *Globe*, one who like himself had seceded from the Saint-Simonian group in 1831, and was now engaged in publicizing in the *Revue Encyclopédique* a socialism that was both religious and democratic; and he introduced her to Pierre Leroux. This friendship which began in 1835 and ended only with Leroux's death in 1871 was the most important of many that the novelist made with contemporary socialists. Several of her novels served to make Leroux's ideas more widely known, and to the same end she created three journals, the *Revue Indépendante*, founded in 1841, the *Éclaireur de l'Indre* (1844–8), and the *Revue Sociale* (1845–50). The novels *Spiridion* (1839), *Consuelo* (1842–3), and *La Comtesse de Rudolstadt* (1843–5) were written in collaboration with him. The drama *Les Sept Cordes de la Lyre* (1839) attempts to illustrate his theory of symbolism. Pierre Leroux (1797–1871), *philosophus hirsutus* as he

[1] *La Ville des Expiations* has been republished in the Bibliothèque Romantique (Belles-Lettres, 1926) with an important preface by A. Rastoul. See also A. J. George, *Pierre Simon Ballanche, Precursor of Romanticism* (Syracuse University Press, 1945); Hunt, *The Epic in XIXth Century France*, chap. iv; A. Viatte, *Les Sources occultes du Romantisme* (Champion, 1928), ii. 214–42.

[2] *Histoire de ma vie*, ii. 180.

was called because of his tousled black hair and general air
of virility, was of all the early socialists the most intimate
with the great Romantic writers. One of the founders of
Le Globe, he was personally familiar with the great ones of
his time in art, in science, and in political affairs, impressing
all who knew him by his learning, his sincerity, and his
goodness of heart. A working mason who met him in 1842
has left this pen-portrait of him in action: 'When Leroux
began tossing his enormous mane of thick, curly hair, and
his eloquent speech lent animation to two large eyes flashing
with intelligence, we remained struck with amazement.
Never had any man I met made such an impression on
me.'[1] To the poets of the period the mystical colour of his
thought made a special appeal, while making him an object
of ridicule to contemporary parodists. Baudelaire hand-
somely reinstates him in *L'Art romantique*, and in *Curiosités esthétiques* vindicates Leroux's ethical interpretation
of Progress in the face of the bourgeois materialism of the
Second Empire.[2] The phraseology of Leroux's early essays
is at times almost Baudelairean, as when he writes:

Aux grandes époques de rénovation, lorsqu'un ordre social
tombe et qu'un monde nouveau va naître, le génie du mal semble
se déchaîner sur la terre.[3]

Leroux was a remarkably intuitive literary critic. His
literary writings made a deep impression at the time they
appeared, and prepared the way for the diffusion of his
social and philosophical ideas. He was at his best, however,
in the criticism of social realities; and the essay of 1831
just quoted, if it made a less universal stir than the *Paroles*

[1] Martin Nadaud, *Mémoires de Léonard, ancien garçon maçon* (Bour-
ganeuf, 1895), 285.
[2] *L'Art romantique* (Calmann-Lévy), 295; *Curiosités esthétiques*,
218–21.
[3] *Revue Encyclopédique*, September 1831.

d'un croyant, had more manifold literary repercussions. It was he who introduced into usage not only the term *socialisme* but the concept *solidarité*, a concept that has firmly established itself in Sociology and in Law.[1] Himself a disciple of Rousseau not less than of Saint-Simon, Leroux was first and foremost a democrat; and while agreeing with Rousseau that no pure democracy ever actually existed, upheld it as a religious ideal and firmly believed in the ultimate establishment of a world democracy. With Comte he shared the belief that the existence of a society supposes above all a 'moral communion', i.e. common loyalties to some universal and transcendent 'common cause'.

If Democracy is not a religion every democratic revolution is a crime.[2]

His definition of the 'common cause' is Rousseau's. He differed profoundly with Saint-Simon in his views on industrialism, and thought that the Saint-Simonians by glorifying the *industriels* aggravated the ills which they set out to cure. Several years before the appearance of the *Communist Manifesto* Leroux speaks of 'fettered nations working under the rod of capitalism'.[3] Some of his utterances on this theme are absolutely Marxist:

Fundamentally, all wealth, all merchandise represents nothing but human labour, a condensation of human sweat.[4]

It is unnecessary to dwell on his political and economic solutions; they matter less than the spirit in which he

[1] The origins of the word itself date from the French Revolution. Fourier's disciples used it of the doctrine of their master: Hugh Doherty, in *False Association and its Remedy* (1841), introduced it into English usage.
[2] *Revue Encyclopédique*, August 1832.
[3] *Malthus et les économistes* (Boussac, 1849), 25. This work first appeared in 1845–6, in the *Revue Sociale*.
[4] Op. cit. 47.

wrote. This is essentially the spirit of the *Discours sur l'inégalité*. Contrary to general belief, Leroux had nothing to do with Hugo's metaphysics; the poet's theory of metempsychosis is in fact drawn in large part from *Terre et Ciel* (1854) by Jean Reynaud, one-time associate editor with Leroux of the *Encyclopédie Nouvelle*, an ambitious experiment in popular education launched in 1834–43 with the collaboration of Le Play, Hippolyte Carnot, Jules Leroux, Pauline Roland, Lacordaire, Pereire, and others. Reynaud's conception of the after-life, which first emerges in the article 'Ciel',[1] drove Leroux to despair. It was responsible for the cooling-off of their relations with each other and for the fact that their joint project was never completed. Leroux's own philosophy is a social idealism; and it is in the sphere of the poet's social thought and of his progressive philosophy of history that its influence on Hugo lies. Leroux died in obscurity during the Commune, his fame not having survived the calculated slander of a Second Empire 'biographer'. George Sand, then aged sixty-seven, followed his corpse on foot to the cemetery. Some words which she wrote in 1848 would serve as a fitting memorial:

Pierre Leroux, ex-printer and type-setter, eloquent writer and audacious thinker; one of the greatest minds and noblest hearts of the nineteenth century, whose simple and devoted life was always laid at the service of the revolution.[2]

In her youth she was also familiar with the ideas of Charles Fourier, in whom Surrealism lately discovered a precursor.[3] Any day in 1835 one might have observed in the streets of Paris an eccentric old gentleman with a yard-stick, gauging frontages. Once a clerk in a drapery store,

[1] *Encyclopédie Nouvelle*, iii (Gosselin, 1837), 601–16.
[2] In *La Vraie République*, 9 April 1848.
[3] André Breton, *Ode à Charles Fourier* (Paris, Fontaine, 1947).

Fourier spent most of his time measuring bolts of cloth before turning his mind to architecture and to schemes for housing an ideal society. Each morning he would issue forth from the shabby lodgings where he lived alone in the Rue Montmartre, his pockets full of scraps intended for the cats of the neighbourhood, and, attended by a feline retinue, would make for the gardens of the Palais Royal. In twenty years his habits never varied. Punctually each day at noon he returned to his garret to meet the millionaire who never appeared with the funds to finance his soaring ambitions.

Fourier, like Saint-Simon, was obsessed with Newton's physics. His psychology and sociology are based on a theory of 'passionate attraction' which held much interest for Enfantin and his followers.[1] He tells of a society in which everyone will rise at 3 a.m. and rush to work with passionate alacrity; we shall all be doing the tasks we find most attractive, all disagreeable and repugnant chores being turned over to 'little hordes' of boys with a mania for dirtiness, mounted on Shetland ponies and dressed in costumes of 400 different colours (little girls, and the good little boys who behave like little girls, will be allowed to stay in bed late and will spend their time seeing to it that nobody uses bad language). 'Industrial armies' will change the earth's climate by intensive cultivation and reap two harvests annually, in May and November. The national debt of Great Britain will be paid off in six months by increased production of eggs, and gardeners will raise

[1] Actually Fourier's early writings antedate Saint-Simon's; but they did not attract attention till after 1830. He made many proselytes among the dissident Saint-Simonians, but there is also evidence to support Engels's view of 'the Enfantin movement' itself as 'Fourierism fraudulently introduced into the School'. *Correspondance de Karl Marx et F. Engels* (Costes, 1931), i. 43. H. Bourgin, *Fourier*, 420. H. Louvancour, *De Henri de Saint-Simon à Charles Fourier*, 160–5 and chaps. viii, ix, xii.

'honest-to-goodness melons' (des melons jamais trom-
peurs). A perpetual aurora borealis will cover the earth,
spreading heat and light and melting the polar ice-caps.
A 'citric boreal acid' emanating from this aurora and
combining with the salt of the sea will turn the ocean
into lemonade. The earth will acquire four new moons,
each more brilliant than the one we now have. When the
globe has been harmoniously organized it will habitually
have 37 million poets the equals of Homer, 37 million
geometricians equivalent to Newton, and 37 dramatists as
good as Molière. This, Fourier is scrupulous to add, is
only an approximate estimate. He admits that his descriptions of the state of the world in association read like fairy-
tales, 'in spite of the care I have taken to avoid a Romantic
tinge'; but it is evident that he did not try very hard, for he
goes on to say: 'To be a devotee of Romanticism is to be
enamoured of *passionate attraction* and the magnificence it
is about to create on this globe. Six hundred thousand
enormous palaces will take the place of the disgusting
cottages in which our villagers live . . .', &c. 'The passions
will form a tremendous orchestra of 800 million characters
and transform the globe into an earthly paradise.'[1]

It would be a mistake, however, to think that method is
altogether wanting in Fourier's madness. Indeed, his work
as a whole is an incredible 'alliance of arithmetic and
wonder'.[2] Like Saint-Simon, and indeed before him, he
foresaw the rise of capitalism; but unlike him detected
weaknesses in the new industrial system: the business
cycles caused by a 'mania for confused production'[3] and
the resultant 'plethoric crises' (depressions due to over-
production). He followed the eighteenth-century physiocrats

[1] *Traité de l'unité universelle* (1822), in *Œuvres*, ii. 173.
[2] Title of the Quatrième Notice, Pt. II, op. cit.
[3] *Œuvres*, vi. 28.

in regarding agriculture as the true source of the wealth of nations. He had a special horror of tradesmen, noting with indignation that on its way from producer to consumer an apple increases in price tenfold. Fourier's socialism is a consumer socialism. It is to the co-operative principle, and not to the State, that he looks for initiative. His chief twentieth-century disciple, Charles Gide (André Gide's uncle), considered him the founder of the co-operative movement; others dispute the title. What he actually proposed was the establishment, on estates comprising some three square miles of land, of profit-sharing associations which he called *phalanges* (phalanxes), each lodged in a *phalanstère* complete with a library, recreation rooms, community kitchen, &c., and housing not less than 1,620 members, since, according to Fourier, humanity presents exactly 810 species of temperaments, male and female, and it seemed to him important to assemble the greatest possible variety of these. One of Fourier's sounder ideas was that change of occupation is a desirable thing. The *phalanstère*, therefore, was subdivided into smaller associations called *séries*, each devoted to a particular branch of production; every associate might be a member of twenty or thirty of these, and during the day devote himself to as many as eight or ten different types of work. The satisfaction of man's innate need for variety and change in work and pleasure is what Fourier calls *la papillonne* (the 'butterfly passion'). Nothing could be more reminiscent of Rousseau than his description of the site of his 'domestic-agricultural Association'. It is laid in 'a countryside provided with a fine stream of water, interspersed with hills and suited to different forms of cultivation'; in the background is a forest, and a large city is 'not far distant, but distant enough to discourage intruders'.[1] Here young and old, men and

[1] Ibid. iv. 427.

maids, rich and poor, grouped according to their sympathies, follow the occupation that best pleases them at the
moment and leave it when they like to indulge in games,
or picnics, or merry dalliance. A drawing by Victor Considerant, Fourier's disciple, in his *Considérations sociales sur
l'Architectonique* (1834), mildly brings to mind the campus
of the University of California. In the foreground some goats
are browsing, and in the middle distance some 'passionate
series' seem to be doing gracefully nothing in particular.

Many Fourierist communities were actually established,
chiefly in the United States where the way had been prepared by Robert Owen. Fourierism was introduced to the
United States by Albert Brisbane, whose *Social Destiny
of Man* appeared in 1840. Brisbane had studied in France
under Fourier in 1834. In 1842 the *New York Tribune*,[1]
then edited by Horace Greeley, placed at his disposal a
column in which for over a year he popularized Fourier's
doctrines. Thus was bestowed upon American journalism
the gift of its first columnist—Albert Brisbane's son, Arthur
Brisbane, continuing the family tradition till his death
in 1936. The direct effect of Brisbane's writings was the
making of a large number of experiments in community-
living all over the United States during the eighteen-
forties. The most famous of these were the North American
Phalanx of New Jersey, which had 112 members and
flourished for 12 years; the Wisconsin Phalanx, consisting
of 32 families settled on 1,800 acres of land; and Brook
Farm in the Commonwealth of Massachusetts. Originally
a Unitarian settlement, Brook Farm was transformed into
a *phalange* in the winter of 1843–4 by Greeley and Brisbane;
others associated with the enterprise were William Henry
Channing, Henry Ward Beecher, George Ripley, Charles
Dana, and Nathaniel Hawthorne. It flourished till 1847,

[1] The *Tribune*'s London correspondent was at one time Karl Marx.

when a disastrous fire brought financial ruin to the association; thereafter, a number of American Fourierists joined
the commune established in Texas by Fourier's disciple
Victor Considerant in 1849, which lasted till the Civil War.
Some important Fourierist papers were published in
the United States. Three dailies: the *New York Tribune*,
the *New York Morning Chronicle*, and the *Evening Post*,
opened their columns to Fourierist propaganda, as did
several reviews, including the Boston *Dial*. *The Phalanx*,
edited by Brisbane, appeared in New York City in 1843–5,
and *The Harbinger*, a weekly, was published first at Brook
Farm, then at New York (1845–9). Among its contributors
were James Russell Lowell, Henry James (father of the
novelist and of the philosopher), and George Sand, whose
socialist novels appeared in English translation in this important journal.

In Russia Fourier's works were widely read in the early
forties; his devotees thought that the ideal framework for
the *phalanstère* was the Russian *mir*. Petrachevski, Fourier's
chief Russian disciple, did attempt to establish one on his
own property, but his efforts were thwarted by the peasants
and he was himself condemned to the Siberian mines.
Certain institutions of the Soviet Union today, the *sovkhoz*
and *kolkhoz*, parallel Fourier's ideas; the Stakhanovite
workers have been compared to his 'industrial athletes'
and the Communist Youth Brigades to his 'petites hordes'.
The Russians were passionately interested in the ideas
not only of Fourier but of the Saint-Simonians and their
disciples: Pierre Leroux in particular influenced, through
Herzen, the socialism of the populist period.[1] No account
of Russian socialism can overlook *Spiridion* and *Consuelo*,
which with the *Revue Encyclopédique* were among the chief
channels of transmission for these influences. Dostoievsky

[1] Raoul Labry, *Alexandre Ivanovič Herzen* (Paris, Bossard, 1928).

testifies in his Diary that George Sand brought to Russia 'an enormous sum of thought, of love, of noble enthusiasms and deep convictions'.[1]

In France, the chief support for Fourier came from the dissident Saint-Simonians; and it is not to Fourier himself but to his disciples Victor Considerant, Just Muiron, Lechevalier, Transon, and Hippolyte Renaud that the doctrine owed its diffusion. Their organized propaganda commenced in 1831, and on 1 June 1832 appeared the first number of *Le Phalanstère*, the earliest Fourierist journal. The most complete exposition of the doctrine is Considerant's *Destinée sociale*, of which the first volume appeared in 1834.

Of George Sand's novels, *Le Péché de M. Antoine* (1845) owes something to Fourier, for it presents in the person of the Marquis de Boisguilbault who leaves four millions to found an agricultural commune the 'deus ex machina' that Fourier had dreamt of all his life and never encountered. Fourier was more of a feminist than George Sand. As Engels remarks, he was the first to consider the degree of feminine emancipation as the criterion of a civilized society.[2] He was, in fact, one of the first to demand careers for women. He writes in 1808 that 'women, given freedom, will surpass men in all functions of mind or body that are not the attribute of physical strength',[3] giving it as his reason that from Semiramis to Catherine the Great we find seven great queens to one mediocre one, whereas we commonly find seven mediocre kings to one great monarch![4] It remains to be said that he was a life-long bachelor.

Other traces of the literary influence of Fourier are met

[1] The best study of George Sand is by a Russian critic, Wladimir Karénine: *George Sand, sa vie et ses œuvres*. The Introduction deals with her fortunes in Russia.   [2] *Anti-Dühring*, iii. 11.

[3] *Théorie des quatre mouvements* (1808), 221.

[4] *Œuvres*, i. 218–19.

with in Leconte de Lisle, who contributed to the paper
La Phalange and whose first poems were entitled *Poèmes
harmoniens*. Resemblances to Fourier's Law of Universal
Analogy have been recognized in Baudelaire's doctrine of
correspondances.[1] Baudelaire in 1848 was associated with
Lamennais on the staff of a socialist newspaper, *La Tribune
nationale*, which till recently has been completely over-
looked.[2] On the third of June he proposed to its readers a
slate of candidates including Proudhon and Pierre Leroux,
in these words: 'If you want noble and courageous de-
fenders, men sincerely devoted to the sacred cause of the
people, nominate men of the people, nominate men who
identify themselves with the people, men ready to fight
and die for its sake.' Sartre has shown how powerfully he
was swept off his feet by undercurrents of the Industrial
Revolution from Saint-Simon to Marx.[3] The tragedy of
Baudelaire's existence, in fact, according to Sartre, was that
he did not permanently commit himself to the 'people's
cause' by the side of Victor Hugo, George Sand, and
Pierre Leroux. But this is to overlook his single-handed
defence, in *L'Art romantique*, of the Romantic metaphysician and of the working-class poets; the social poems
dedicated to Hugo in the *Fleurs du mal*; the concluding
poem, *Le Voyage*, which pays an implicit tribute to
social romanticism; and the critique of the new industrial
world inherent in the whole book:

> Ses yeux polis sont faits de minéraux charmants,
> Et dans cette nature étrange et symbolique
> Où tout n'est qu'or, acier, lumière et diamants,
> Resplendit à jamais, comme un astre inutile,
> La froide majesté de la femme stérile.

[1] J. Pommier, *La Mystique de Baudelaire*, 65–68.
[2] J. Mouquet and W. T. Bandy, *Baudelaire en 1848: La Tribune
nationale* (Émile-Paul, 1946).
[3] J. P. Sartre, *Baudelaire* (N.R.F., 1947), 118–19.

Like Marx, the author of the *Fleurs du mal* had a special faculty for perceiving what Leroux called 'le génie du mal déchaîné sur la terre'; and granting that the poet was responsible, as Sartre says, for his *vie de raté*, it is no less true that his work constitutes an 'engagement' of the highest order, for it negates a negation.

The works of George Sand are a common meeting-ground for many diverse influences. Renan sums up the matter well when he says:

Her works are truly the echo of our age, and she will be loved when this age is no more. . . . The world she lived in never received a wound from which her heart did not bleed, never suffered a malady that failed to wring from her harmonious words of sympathy. Her books . . . will for ever be a witness of all that we have hoped for, thought, felt, and suffered.[1]

During the Second Republic she was closely associated with the journalistic activities of Louis Blanc. Like many of his contemporaries, including Marx, Louis Blanc found inspiration in the French Revolution, which suggested to him the conception of an authority to reform society by legislative means. He brought to the forefront the vital issue of labour-organization and popularized the principle of an organizing State. In his *Organisation du travail* (1839) he proposes the establishment with State encouragement of workers' co-operatives, as a first step towards the socialization of capital. The abolition of the wage-system and the absorption of individual capital into social capital are the end-results for which his programme of 'social workshops' was designed; the 'national workshops' of 1848 bear not the slightest resemblance to his ideas—in fact they were deliberately set up to discredit him and to provide a reserve labour force that could be used to put down popular

[1] Quoted by Leblond in *RSoc.*, xl. 190, from Renan's *Feuilles détachées*.

risings. Beyond economic solutions Louis Blanc envisaged a total regeneration of man and of social relationships, and was convinced that it could be achieved by forethought and not by violence. Intellectualism is marked in some of his telling phrases. 'It is not force that governs the world, in spite of appearances. It is thought.'[1] 'The true history of our age is the history of its ideas.'[2] Instead of appealing to the class-war he appeals to harmony and unity; and in this respect he is as Romantic as George Sand. As with Leroux, universal suffrage is for him the instrument of social regeneration. The class-struggle being, in his conception, the result of ignorance, he pins his hopes to the co-operation of labour and capital under the leadership of science; and his socialism consists, as he himself puts it, of 'regularizing and moralizing the activities of society, and rescuing the government of human affairs from the grip of chance'.[3]

More revolutionary and not less Romantic is the figure of Louis-Auguste Blanqui, a 'temperament supercharged with the electricity of his time', as Lamartine says. No tourist will ever know the Mont Saint-Michel as well as he did. The lovely medieval abbey was in those days an island fortress, its approaches being forbidden to all vessels save the sailing-ship *L'Espoir*, whose ironic function it was to revictual the penitentiary. Imprisoned there in 1840 for organizing armed rebellion, Blanqui had from his cell-window a view of the Tour de la Liberté and of the prison grave-yard; and there he wrote a book on *Eternity in the Stars*. A student of law and medicine, Blanqui had joined the illegal *carbonaro* society at the age of eighteen, and was for some time a shorthand reporter on the staff

[1] *Histoire de la Révolution Française* (1842 edition), i. 90–91.
[2] *Histoire de dix ans* (1844 edition), iii. 89.
[3] *Questions d'aujourd'hui et de demain*, ii. 118–19.

of *Le Globe;* in 1834 he brought out a paper of his own, *Le Libérateur*, 'journal des opprimés voulant une Réforme sociale par la République'. Blanqui played a leading part in the affairs of the Société des Amis du Peuple, and, with his fellow conspirator Barbès, organized the equally illegal Société des Saisons. He did not agree with Louis Blanc that thought governs the world. He believed in action. Thirty-three and a half years of his life were spent in jail, ten and a half years in exile; yet his courage never faltered. Twice he was condemned to death and subsequently pardoned. The Monarchy of July interned him at Versailles, Paris, Fontevrault, Mont Saint-Michel, and Blois; the Second Republic sent him to the Fortress of Vincennes; during the Second Empire he spent seven years at the penitentiary of Belle-Ile off the coast of Brittany and then was deported to Corsica and Algeria; and at the age of sixty-six, during the Commune, he was locked up for eight months in a cell seven and a half feet long by four and a half wide. Treated under all forms of government with the inhumanity meted out to political prisoners in our own day, Blanqui, or 'l'Enfermé' as he came to be called, became a mythical figure, the incarnation of the revolutionary tradition of Babeuf and Buonarroti.[1]

Blanqui, Pierre Leroux, and Louis Blanc are often called by their contemporaries 'communists'. As Engels explains in the third preface to the *Communist Manifesto*, the word 'communist' originally referred to the working-class movement, as distinguished from the ideologies of Fourier, Saint-Simon, and Robert Owen, which were then known as 'socialism'. Written later than 1848, the *Manifesto*, he adds, would have been called the 'Socialist Mani-

[1] Maurice Dommanget, *Blanqui* (Librairie de l'Humanité, 1924); Gustave Geffroy, *L'Enfermé* (Crès, 1926, 2 vols.); Sylvain Molinier, *Blanqui* (Presses Universitaires, 1948).

festo'. Heine noticed that most of the workmen with whom
he talked on his visits to the proletarian quarters of Paris
in the early eighteen-forties were communists;[1] it has been
estimated that by the end of 1847 there were no fewer than
200,000 of them in the country, and police reports of the
period have been published bearing testimony to their
activities at Lyons and elsewhere, and to the nervousness
of the authorities.[2] Marx, who became a communist in
Paris in 1844, declares quite accurately that 'Communism
is not of German, but of British and French origin'.
Sainte-Beuve speaks of the 'communism' of George Sand
and Pierre Leroux as early as 1841. The word was of
recent coinage: it is first used by Étienne Cabet, in an
article of 1840 entitled 'Le Démocrate devenu communiste
malgré lui'.[3] The following year the *Revue Indépendante*
devoted an article to the subject of communism.[4] It defines
communist as 'a supporter of equality in industrial society,
that is, an enemy of the present-day economic set-up and
of the usurpation which the law is supposed to consecrate
for the benefit of the upper classes'; but it denounces the
communist ideology as a political form of pantheism in
which Christian reverence for the personality gives way
to authoritarianism: in a sense, says the writer, Prime
Minister Guizot when he sends people to the poor-house
or to prison, and conscripts them for the army, is prac-
tising communism.

It is a fact little realized today that if France is the

---

[1] *Lutezia*: appendix 'Kommunismus, Philosophie und Kleriserei',
in *Sämtliche Werke* (Inselverlag), vol. ix.

[2] G. Bourgin, 'Documents inédits sur la propagande icarienne de
1840 à 1844', *RSoc*, xlvi (1907), 519–41.

[3] G. Morange, *Les Idées communistes dans les sociétés secrètes et dans
la presse de la Monarchie de Juillet* (Paris, 1905).

[4] Jacques Dupré, 'Du Communisme', *Revue Indépendante*, i (December 1841), 337–48.

'classic land of socialism' the United States contests with
Russia the claim to be considered the classic land of
communism. The story of the communists in America,
where they were then known as Primitive Christians, is
one of the most incredible in the history of Utopias.
Cabet's writings made thousands of converts among the
working class, especially skilled workers, while Saint-
Simonism appealed rather to intellectuals and technicians,
and Fourierism to retired officers, civil servants, lawyers,
and petits bourgeois. Many French workmen came to
believe in the real existence of the dream-city of Icaria,[1]
and Cabet was driven to attempt to create it *de toutes
pièces*. Arriving at New Orleans on 27 March 1848, an
advance guard sailed up the Mississippi to Shreveport, and
thence headed by ox-wagon for a concession of land pur-
chased by Cabet in London from a promotion-company.
Of its exact location he had himself only the vaguest idea:
in an Icarian Almanac for 1848 he places it in Oklahoma,
near a town now called Eldorado; actually it lay in the
middle of the wilderness, in Texas.

> Chaque îlot signalé par l'homme de vigie
> Est un Eldorado promis par le Destin;
> L'Imagination qui dresse son orgie
> Ne trouve qu'un récif aux clartés du matin.[2]

After suffering many perils and privations the explorers
beat a retreat to New Orleans. Cabet having joined them
there the following year, a fresh start was made at Nauvoo
(Illinois) on the site of the former Mormon settlement.
Here the Icarians remained for several years, joined by
new arrivals from France: altogether, 496 people emigrated.
In 1856 the first serious schism occurred. Cabet, whose

---

[1] *Voyage en Icarie, roman philosophique et social* (1839).
[2] Baudelaire, *Le Voyage*.

rule was absolute and dictatorial, passed sumptuary laws which made him increasingly unpopular with the majority. He prohibited the use of tobacco and liquor, allowing the men only a tot of whisky before going to work in the morning. Cabet's was the only prohibition legislation that has ever been successful in the United States; his secret was simple: he gave his subjects no money with which to get drunk. It was further decreed that there should be no variations in feminine fashions. Of women's hats there were to be only a limited number of standard styles, and to avoid any nonsense with sizes each hat must be expansible and contractible at will. It should here be mentioned that Cabet's wife and daughter did not accompany him to America. Finally, removed from the Presidency, he left for St. Louis, Missouri, where he died in 1856. For some time those who remained loyal to him cultivated an estate six miles from St. Louis, across the Mississippi at Cheltenham, while the majority, who had remained at Nauvoo, moved in 1860 to Corning, Iowa. There they were joined in 1867 by Jules Leroux, Pierre Leroux's brother, who with his sons came to the United States that year and published at Corning a French-language newspaper, *L'Étoile du Kansas et de l'Iowa*, devoted to the doctrine of the editor of *Le Globe*. In the spring of 1881 the Leroux family moved west to California, and, at Cloverdale, Sonoma County, created a colony which they called Speranza in memory of Pierre Leroux, whose last journalistic enterprise was the review *L'Espérance*. A ranch known as the Bluxome Ranch, on the Russian River two and a half miles south of Cloverdale on the way to Healdsburg and San Francisco, was owned by the joint-stock company Icaria-Speranza-Commune and proved a financial success. Jules Leroux, militant socialist of the eighteen-thirties, lies buried in the soil of California, where he died in 1883. The Iowa community broke up in 1898. Nothing is left of them but a few ruins on the shores of the Mississippi, a few deserted shacks on the wind-swept prairie; these, and a line of Baudelaire meaningless to all who have not heard their story:

Notre âme est un trois-mâts cherchant son Icarie.

Cabet's communism was, as George Sand says, 'essentially peaceful and inoffensive'.[1] The *Crédo communiste* holds that 'democracy cannot be organized by violence, and that no victorious minority can impose it upon the majority'.[2] With the enactment of universal suffrage as a necessary preliminary, society, Cabet maintained, would attain by legitimate means its new economic basis in common ownership, with a guarantee to all, in return for a moderate amount of labour, of a place to live, the means of sustenance, security against accident and disaster, and the right to marry and raise a family. And he emphasized that the progress of industry made such a goal attainable; in fact, he looked forward to a development of the use of machinery to a point at which 'le rôle de l'homme se borne à être directeur des machines'.[3] He differed from Marx in thinking that it was possible for communists to isolate themselves from the rest of society: Icarian communism, to Marx, was merely a form of escapism, and Cabet should have remained in Europe and participated in the class-struggle.

An important aspect of George Sand's own 'communism' is the encouragement which she gave to working-class writers. In the *Revue Indépendante* of January 1842 she devotes a lengthy article to the *Poésies sociales des*

---

[1] *La Vraie République*, 7 May 1848.
[2] *Crédo communiste* (Prévot, 1841), 13.
[3] Op. cit. 10–11.

ouvriers just published by Olinde Rodrigues, Saint-Simon's secretary.[1] The development of a working-class literature constitutes a feature of the Romantic period which is truly revolutionary, representing as it does the first beginnings of the proletarian literature of the present day.[2] 'Of the writers of the period who gave a sympathetic welcome to working-class authors, one showed greater insight into their soul and spirit than any others, and that was George Sand.'[3] One of her own writings was directly influenced by their works: the *Livre du Compagnonnage* (1839) of Agricol Perdiguier Museux, one-time joiner's apprentice and later Représentant du Peuple, is the source of her *Compagnon du Tour de France* (1840), an eloquent denunciation of the social caste-system and eulogy of proletarian idealism, which the *Revue des Deux Mondes* refused to print. George Eliot's *Adam Bede* (1858) is a reincarnation of the hero of this novel, Pierre Huguenin.

The origins of the working-class press also go back to the Romantic period. In France as in Great Britain, 1830 marks the appearance of the first newspapers published by and for workmen; the most important are Cabet's *Le Populaire*, 'journal des intérêts politiques, matériels et moraux du Peuple' (1833–5 and 1841–51), and *L'Atelier*, edited by Buchez, among his associates being the working-class poets Magu, Poncy, and Eugène Pottier, author of the 'Internationale'.[4]

Contemporaneously with George Sand's scandalous novel there appeared in 1840 a work by an unknown

[1] 'Dialogue familier sur la poésie des prolétaires', *Revue Indépendante*, ii. 37–65.

[2] See Prof. Dolléans's preface to my *Socialisme romantique*. H. J. Hunt devotes a chapter of *Le Socialisme et le Romantisme en France* to the proletarian poets.

[3] Dolléans, *Histoire du mouvement ouvrier*, i. 197.

[4] A. Cuvillier, *Un journal d'ouvriers: 'L'Atelier'* (Alcan, 1919).

writer, entitled *Qu'est-ce que la propriété?* and giving the
equally scandalous answer: 'La propriété, c'est le vol.'
Pierre-Joseph Proudhon was once described by George
Sand as 'le plus grand ennemi du Socialisme';[1] but, using
the term in the sense which it then had, in the same breath
she could go on to say that he had done great service to
the cause of the people. His thought matured only after
1848 and thus exerted no influence upon the Romantic
writers; but throughout the Second Empire, in the face
of a society intoxicated with prosperity and pleasure,
Proudhon alone made the voice of justice heard, and did
so with the sternness and anger of the Old Testament
prophets. He is sometimes quoted as saying that all Romantic books should be thrown into the fire.[2] He would
certainly have spared from the flames the works of Michelet, the metaphysics of whose Introduction (1847) to the
Histoire de la Révolution Française is systematized in his
own masterpiece, *De la Justice dans la Révolution et dans
l'Église* (1858). When Michelet writes: 'Je définis la Révolution l'avènement de la Loi, la résurrection du Droit, la
réaction de la Justice', he speaks for Proudhon as well as
for Romanticism. And in a fragment written the same
year as his *Principe de l'art* Proudhon himself detects
in the works of George Sand and in Hugo's *Misérables*
signs of an 'original literature to come'. '*Les Misérables*
has accents that penetrate, unlike any work of the past,
. . . something to grip crowds as no one had ever done
before.'[3]

Like the Romantic philosophies of history, Proudhon's
thought is progressive.

The true in all things, the real, is that which changes . . .,

---

[1] *Correspondance*, iii (1882), 340–1, letter to Mazzini.
[2] *Du principe de l'art* (Garnier, 1865), 63.
[3] Daniel Halévy, *La Vie de Proudhon*, 444.

while the false, the fictitious, is anything that presents itself as fixed and unalterable.[1]

Like the thought of Hegel and of Marx in particular, its character is dialectical, proceeding as it does from the perception of contradictions inherent in reality by the method of confronting 'opposites' (antinomies). The same principle underlies the aesthetics of the *Préface de Cromwell*. With Hegel, the dialectical progression follows a ternary rhythm; the Romantic philosophy is a transcendental or absolute idealism. Proudhon's system, on the other hand, is one of immanence: 'the antinomy is not resolved; the two terms of which it is composed *balance* each other'.[2] He does not conceive of this equilibrium as something fixed and unalterable, but as something becoming. From the tensions of experience emerge progressively, in life, intelligence and consciousness; and these are the Proudhonian absolute. In the social sphere, the term used to express the balance is *justice*. In political life, the corresponding term is *federalism*; in economic life, *mutuality*, i.e. reciprocal exchange of services, takes the place of class oppositions.

Marx and Engels hoped at one time to gain the support of Proudhon and of the leading Chartists, and Marx wrote to Proudhon in 1846 inviting him to join their association. Proudhon's reply was characteristic. He objected to the dogmatic tone of the communists, dwelt on the dangers of intolerance, and warned Marx against following the example of his compatriot Luther. The revolutionary method he rejected outright, denouncing it as contrary to the ends of communism.

Let us wage good, honest polemics; let us set the world an example of wise and foreseeing tolerance, but let us not,

---

[1] *Philosophie du progrès* (Marcel Rivière), 50–51.
[2] *De la Justice* . . . (Marcel Rivière), ii. 155. Proudhon's italics.

because we are at the head of a movement, make ourselves the leaders of a new intolerance, let us not set ourselves up as apostles of a new religion, though it be the religion of logic and of reason. Let us welcome and encourage all manner of dissent . . .; never regard any question as finally settled, and when we have worn out our very last argument begin all over again, if need be, with eloquence and irony. On these terms I shall be pleased to enter your association, otherwise not.[1]

'Ironie, vraie liberté! . . . Maîtresse de vérité!' It was Proudhon's distinction among the socialists of his time that he possessed, or rather was possessed by, the ironic spirit. 'What our generation needs', he writes, 'is not a Mirabeau, a Robespierre, or a Bonaparte, but a Voltaire. . . . Liberty, like reason, exists and manifests itself only by continuing contempt of its own works; it perishes when it descends to self-adulation. . . . Stationary peoples are all solemn peoples.'[2]

A Romantic feature in his writings is the 'burning patience' with which he devoted himself to the task of making men and society reasonable.[3] For of him too, in the last analysis, it might be said, as of George Sand: *Il faut être passionné*. In his advocacy of justice Proudhon is uncompromising, for he believed with a religious conviction that our purpose in life is not merely to make a living but 'to reproduce within us the Divine likeness and bring to pass on earth the Kingdom of the Spirit; to be men, and rise above the contingencies of Fate'.[4] This is why he spent many years in exile or in prison, and why in the polite society of his day the very name of Proudhon was anathema.

Finally we come to a name which one never hears

[1] *Correspondance* (Lacroix, 1875), ii. 198 ff.

[2] *Confessions d'un révolutionnaire* (Garnier, 1849), 292–3.

[3] 'Et à l'aurore, armés d'une ardente patience, nous entrerons aux splendides villes.' Rimbaud, *Une Saison en enfer*.

[4] Quoted by Dolléans in his *Proudhon*, 323.

mentioned today. It is the name of the apostle of collectivism and of socialization, Constantin Pecqueur (1801–
1887). For some time associated with the left wing of the
Saint-Simonian movement, Pecqueur wrote for *Le Globe*
but rebelled against Enfantin's theocracy and turned for
some time to Fourierism. His religious ideas are akin to
those of Buchez and Leroux, while politically it is natural
to associate him with Vidal[1] and Louis Blanc, who sat
with him in 1848 on the Commission du Luxembourg.
His *Économie sociale des intérêts du commerce, de l'industrie,
de l'agriculture et de la civilisation en général* appeared in
1836. It is a little startling to find that this book, 'the
first socialist treatise founded on economic science',[2] was
awarded a prize of 1,500 francs by the Académie des
Sciences Morales et Politiques; it was written in reply to
a question set for competition by that learned body, which
was preoccupied with the moral and material influence of
railroads and of steam machinery. On that subject Pecqueur's confident optimism marks a contrast with Vigny's
anxiety in *La Maison du berger*; nevertheless, in their fundamental outlook poet and economist are at one, for both
speak of a society which by the processes of industrialism
is working towards the goal of 'association'.

With his love of generous ideas, at times a little
extravagant and hazy, Pecqueur was, as one of his biographers has characterized him, a typical son of the
Romantic age.[3] And yet he was the first to expound in

---

[1] François Vidal (1814–72), author of *De la répartition des riches-
ses ou de la justice distributive en économie sociale* (Paris, Capelle, 1846)
and *Vivre en travaillant! projets, voies et moyens de réformes sociales*
(Paris, Capelle, 1848), advocated community housing and the establishment of credit institutions and 'agricultural colonies' to combat
pauperism.

[2] Fournière, *Le Règne de Louis-Philippe*, 474.

[3] G. Marcy, *Constantin Pecqueur*, 256–7.

detail a collectivist system. Marx quotes twice in *Das Capital*[1] from his *Théorie nouvelle d'économie sociale et politique* (1842). Pecqueur's influence is also perceptible in the *Communist Manifesto*. It will be recalled that the nationalization of land, the abolition of the right of inheritance, and the centralization of credit were part of the Saint-Simonian programme; two other items in the *Manifesto*, the centralization of transport in the hands of the State and the unification of agricultural labour with industrial, were advocated by Pecqueur. But above all Marx drew from Pecqueur elements of his historical materialism: his description of the progressive contamination of society by the methods and morals of capitalism; his analysis of the process whereby small business enterprise is gradually squeezed out by the merciless competition of big combines (Pecqueur considers it an 'important industrial phenomenon' that 'the whole mechanism of the production and circulation of wealth is being controlled by an infinitely smaller number of leaders', and speaks in this connexion of 'monopoly');[2] and his prediction of imperialist wars as a probable (Marx will say, a necessary) consequence of the new system. Pecqueur was struck by 'unmistakable signs of world-wide revolution in the industrial, political and moral spheres'.[3] He foresaw that soon workers would be 'assembled by the hundreds in vast establishments, and subjected to such punctuality in service, such perfection in workmanship, and such industrial order and discipline as nothing in the mechanism of labour and production today can give any conception of'.[4] Politically, these new conditions of production could lead, he thought, in liberal countries, either to the association of the middle class and a minority of wage-earners or to a 'feudalism' in commerce

[1] Book I, chap. 12.
[2] *Économie sociale*, i. 270.
[3] Op. cit. i. 274.
[4] Op. cit. i. 271–2.

and industry with its obligatory accompaniment of a large-scale proletariat. In countries politically less evolved, small capitalists would be ground down to the level of the proletariat by monopoly-capitalism, which is 'feudalism with its countless proletarians attached to the industrial sod, its small middle class and few free artisans'; 'small industry disappears with its small employers—there is monopoly, and society is really composed of two great classes: the toiling multitudes, and the great businessmen and great entrepreneurs'.[1] The association of small enterprises offered, according to him, one of the best means of 'socializing' property.[2] It leads to what he calls 'pure industrial democracy'.[3] What Pecqueur, however, actually advocated was a compromise solution, a combination of industrial democracy and large-scale private enterprise, on the grounds that it would tend to that 'fusion of classes' which is George Sand's dream in all her novels, and avoid the 'despair-breeding and antisocial monotony of absolute equality, or of an aristocratic ascendancy which would crush and dominate the masses'.[4] The fact is that his attitude to political democracy is distinctly suspicious: he speaks of it as a wilderness'.[5] But towards vested interests he is still more severe. He does not hesitate to say that a considerable portion of the governing classes, landed aristocracy, merchants, and manufacturers, is 'impious and branded with capital guilt by the higher justice of the moral law which governs the Christian world'. 'Fanatically attached to their possessions and their interests, everywhere in the two worlds they are as harsh and intractable

[1] Op. cit. i. 274–6.
[2] 'La socialisation pro ressive des sources de la richesse, des instruments de travail, des conditions du bien-être universel.' Op. cit. i, p. xii.
[3] Op. cit. i. 278.   [4] Ibid.
[5] Op. cit. i. 289. Cf. Vigny's 'un désert de sables' (Les Oracles).

as the miser huddled over his threatened treasure. They
have lost the sense of the social, and remembered only
those moral prescriptions which lend themselves to the
service of selfish interests.'[1] And writing in his paper *Le
Salut du Peuple* (1849–50) an article entitled 'Le Progrès
par la Douleur', in which occurs the word *collectivisme*,
Pecqueur addresses these reflections to contemporary
statesmen:

You will not succeed in your endeavours to whitewash the
great ruin of feudal society by means of transitory expedients.
. . . Remember the fates of so many famous nations: Rome,
Greece, Egypt, Assyria. . . . Take heed lest civilization plant
her banners on the summit of the Kremlin—lest she give her
baptism of predilection to the countless race of the Slavs! Take
heed! Immortality is promised only to those nations which
militate for progress, for liberty, equality, and fraternity all over
the world. France today has reached a solemn and formidable
moment at which the question before her is set in these terms:
To be or not to be, death or radical transformation.[2]

Prophetic words! Towards the middle of the century
the term 'socialism' became synonymous with the working-
class movement launched, not by Karl Marx, but by the
forgotten militants of the thirties and forties in Great
Britain and France who founded the first trade unions.

Syndicalism, whose theorician Georges Sorel was a
disciple of Proudhon, is sometimes represented as continuing the revolutionary tradition of the Romantics
while Marxism is said to follow the scientific tradition of
Positivism.[3] This distinction overlooks many Romantic
affinities to be found both in Auguste Comte and in Marx.

Romanticism is defined as the literature of individual-

[1] *Économie sociale*, i. 291.
[2] *Le Salut du Peuple*, 10 April 1850, p. 7.
[3] É. Halévy, *Histoire du socialisme européen*, 234.

ism; but the relation in terms between the individual and the social is as much misunderstood by Marxist as by bourgeois critics. If we may believe a schoolboy's essay of 1835 on the choice of a career, 'it would be a mistake to think that these two interests are necessarily opposed and that one must destroy the other'. The schoolboy who wrote this composition was Marx, and he enlarges on the point in 1844: 'We must avoid setting up 'society' as an abstraction in the face of the individual. The individual *is* the social being. . . . The individual life and the generic life of man are not different.'[1] This is almost exactly Hugo's theme in the Preface to his *Contemplations*. Twenty-four years earlier, reviewing his *Feuilles d'Automne*, the *Globe* had noticed the presence within 'this entirely individualist poetry' of 'a deep-seated sense of humanity', and made the comment: 'Man is not sufficient unto himself, for the great artist needs the whole of humanity as his family. . . . *Personality* is not to be sacrificed to *socialism*, nor socialism to personality: the harmonization of both these aspects of man's life is the purpose of all our efforts.'[2]

A collective interest in the middle ages focused Marx's attention on the struggles of the guilds in medieval Italy and Flanders, just as it moved George Sand to interest herself in the arts and crafts of medieval and Renaissance Italy, or Pierre Leroux to investigate medieval heresies. Like Michelet again, Marx at the beginning of his career was fascinated by the French Revolution, and was under its spell when he wrote the *Communist Manifesto*. Like

---

[1] Quoted in M. Rubel, *Karl Marx: pages choisies pour une éthique socialiste* (Marcel Rivière, 1948), 3, 323. The sociological implications of these texts are developed by Gurvitch in *CIS.*, iv (1948), 22ff.

[2] *Globe*, 13 February 1832. Though this article antedates by two years Leroux's historic opposition of 'individualism and socialism', the context shows clearly that by 'socialism' the writer (Joncières) means what today we should call 'le social'.

the Romantic poets, thinkers, and composers, he viewed
history in a dramatic light, and it is the Promethean
quality of his work, at least as much as the scientific, that
has made his name so awe-inspiring.

'Le combat ou la mort; la lutte sanguinaire ou le néant.
C'est ainsi que la question est invinciblement posée.'[1] With
these words of George Sand's Marx closes his reply to
Proudhon (1847). After spending over a year in Paris,
where he interested himself in the affairs of German workmen, Marx sought to achieve by force a 'social order in
which political revolution shall give way to social evolution',[2] and to this end helped to organize the International
Working Men's Association. 'Force is the midwife of
every old society pregnant with a new one.' Proudhon
believed in social regeneration by justice; he devoted his
life to the struggle for legislation designed to safeguard the
dignity of the individual in the new industrial age. The
Romantic school sought a transcendental solution the
reverse of Marx's: regeneration through universal love.
'Pardonnez-moi, ô Justice, je vous ai crue austère et
dure, et je n'ai pas vu que vous étiez la même chose que
l'Amour et que la Grâce.'[3] Not one of these solutions is
psychologically unrealistic; and it should not be forgotten
that Engels held the 'Utopian socialists' (as he was the
first to call them) in the highest regard. In the works of
Saint-Simon, and in those of Fourier and Owen, Engels
recognizes ideas of true genius which the 'literary grocers',
as he calls their critics, are incapable of understanding.[4]
Writing recently in the *Revue philosophique* on Proudhon
and Michelet, an eminent contemporary sociologist ob-

[1] *Misère de la philosophie* (Giard edition), 244.   [2] Ibid.
[3] Michelet, *Histoire de la Révolution Française*, Introduction, i.
123-4.
[4] *Utopian and Scientific Socialism* (Paris, Bureau d'éditions, 1936),
45.

serves that the transcendentalism of Marx and that of
the Romantics correspond each to real energies within the
élan vital, which is indissolubly compounded of selfishness
and affection, will to power and self-sacrifice, antagonism
and generosity.[1] It would indeed be difficult to discover
economic motivation for the life of a philosopher like
Marx, or to deny in the light of history that, as Professor
Laski says, 'Communism has made its way by its idealism
and not its realism'. In Proudhon's principle of justice
M. Guy-Grand recognizes a third vital force: the force of
reason; and he thinks that the future depends upon the
balance which the third force may hold between the apostles
of violence and those who believe in world brotherhood
and democratic solidarity. Such ideas are today in the
ascendancy in Europe; and there can be no doubt of the
aptitude and inclination of the western European nations
to play the Proudhonian role. But Proudhon's reason led
him to the conviction, expressed in his maturest work,
that the only way out of a world in process of dissolution
was through a total revolution of our thinking and social
behaviour;[2] and in this there is no division between him
and the Romantics. The question therefore arises: shall
we not merely set up a third force, but improve on suspicion, hatred, and violence? If the answer is no, the
Proudhonian solution will be inoperative and Marx may
have the last word.

Proudhon, as has been said, was a federalist; and his
views carry much weight today with the architects of
Western Union. The 'national socialisms' with which we
have become only too familiar are abhorrent to the tradition of a hundred years. All the early socialists agree that
the individual is the end, and not the State. Pecqueur, who

[1] Georges Guy-Grand in *Rph*, cxxxviii (December 1948), 385–408.
[2] Dolléans, *Proudhon*, 293.

gives the State an importance greater than that accorded
to it by most of his contemporaries, and whose powerfully centralized and authoritative government would have
powers as extensive as those of the most absolute monarch,[1]
denounces those who would explain the evolution of society
without reference to the wills of individuals. Jean Reynaud
writes in criticism of Plato's *Republic*:

However great one may conceive society to be, the citizen is
fundamentally greater, for in the reality of his being he contains the principle of a development infinite in nature, from
which all earthly institutions are necessarily excluded. . . .
Hence a political system based on a multiplicity and a com-
plexity of relations is an achievement incomparably more
admirable in the skilful harmony of its functioning than the
State of the Greek philosopher, with its elementary sym-
metries. The ideal republic is a union of happy families.[2]

The Encyclopedists consider it the function of the State,
first to 'ensure the material existence of individuals' and
'distribute them to the employments best suited to their
destinies as well as to its own . . . , always being mindful
of the principle that, in the determination of temporal
destinies not less than of man's eternal destiny, power
belongs to persuasion'. And they specify three important
conditions which must be observed if the organizing State
is to be effective: (1) Society must work to a conscious
plan; (2) the State must realize that it is dealing with
individuals, and must try to understand their psychology;
(3) the morality of public servants and their personal
disinterestedness must be above reproach.[3] In an article
on 'Adam Smith', Jules Leroux derives from the principles

[1] Marcy, *Constantin Pecqueur*, 71.

[2] 'Famille', *Encyclopédie Nouvelle*, v (1839), 198–9.

[3] Jean Reynaud, 'Souveraineté', *Encyclopédie Nouvelle*, viii (1841),
249.

of individualism the conclusion that the function of the State is essentially to 'harmonize the relations of the individual and society', and speaks of its authority as an educative, even more than an organizing and judicial, authority.[1] Proudhon is much the strongest individualist. He regards the State as an octopus which must be destroyed if man is to be free.

To be GOVERNED is to be kept under close watch, inspected, spied upon, managed, legislated, regimented, corralled, indoctrinated, preached at, rubber-stamped, evaluated, adjudged, found fault with, ordered about, by beings who have neither title, nor knowledge, nor virtue. . . . To be GOVERNED is at each operation, at every transaction, every movement, to be ticketed, registered, checked and double-checked, docketed, measured, priced, assessed, licensed, patented, warranted, postscripted, admonished, impeded, reformed, straightened out and corrected. It is, under pretext of public utility and in the name of the public interest, to be subjected to taxation, trained, ransomed, exploited, monopolized, extorted, squeezed, spoofed and robbed; and then, at the slightest resistance, at the first word of complaint, repressed, fined, vilified, annoyed, persecuted, rough-housed, beaten to death, disarmed, throttled, imprisoned, shot, shelled, judged, condemned, deported, sacrificed, sold out, betrayed, and for full measure fooled, clowned, outraged and dishonoured. That is Government, that is its justice, that is its ethics![2]

Marx did not identify the good of society with the interests of the State. On the contrary he looked forward to a gradual 'withering away' of the attributes of government in the classless society of the future. There is a danger that the crisis through which we are passing, marked, as are all periods of crisis, by the hegemony of the State, may lead us to confuse the purposes of society

[1] *Encyclopédie Nouvelle*, viii (1841), 189-90.
[2] *Idée générale de la Révolution* (Rivière), 344.

with political and economic means devised to meet emer-
gencies: the dictatorship of the proletariat, on the one
hand, or government by decree-laws and orders in council,
on the other. Our times have their limitations, including
an unhappy tendency towards isolationism in time. It is
wholesome, therefore, for us in our anxieties to remember
our solidarity with men and women of a hundred years
ago who faced problems not essentially different from ours
in a broad spirit of humanism. This is the spirit which
George Sand shares with Reynaud, who in the *Revue
Encyclopédique* of 1832 made the first historic appeal for
parliamentary representation of the proletariat, anticipating by forty-seven years the Workers' Party formed by
Jules Guesde;[1] with the printer Jules Leroux, who in
1833 called for 'bonds to unite us', putting forward a
programme of working-class 'solidarity' based on collective
wage-contracts, mutual aid and relief, and the creation of
a co-operative press;[2] and with the Romantic novelist and
militant organizer of the Union Ouvrière, Flora Tristan
(Gauguin's grandmother), who claimed descent from
Montezuma and was one of those who laid the foundations
of the International. The ideology of the social movement was no pipe-dream of a solitary philosopher, it arose
out of the real experience of the common people of France
and Great Britain.

The workers, whatever their trade, . . . are all instruments
of fortune in the hands of their masters. Our common sufferings brought us together. . . . Our class is inexistent, we are
only individuals. Our only hope is in ourselves.[3]

[1] 'De la nécessité d'une représentation spéciale pour les prolétaires', *Revue Encyclopédique*, vol. liv (Apr.–June 1832).
[2] *Aux ouvriers typographes, de la nécessité de fonder une Association
ayant pour but de rendre les ouvriers propriétaires des instruments de
travail* (Paris, Herhan, 1833, 15 pp.). The word 'solidarité' occurs
on p. 5.   [3] Jules Leroux, op. cit. 9–11.

Writing in the *National* of 21 July 1832 with reference to the *Revue Encyclopédique*, Sainte-Beuve expresses the conviction that beneath the spiritual anguish of the times the groundwork is being laid for notable progress in industrial relations, and that this will come as the result of workers' co-operatives, and not from the 'jugglery of our financiers' and their 'art of grouping figures'.[1] In fact he goes farther, and agrees with Leroux and Reynaud that 'without the political guarantees and liberties for which we are having to fight every day, an efficient industrial organization can neither be established nor bear fruit'.[2] The Romantic spirit, indeed, worked as profound changes in economics and political science as it did in history, literature, and the arts. The general nature of the transformation is adequately defined in Victor Hugo's words when he speaks, in 1834, of the 'substitution of social questions for political questions'. Instead of being an abstract theory of government, political science came increasingly to be a science of the governed: in other words, a social science.

The term is used by Bazard as early as 1825.[3] It occurs prominently in the March 1833 number of the *Revue Encyclopédique*, in an article on 'Political Economy considered as a Science'.—'What is the practical purpose of political economy?' asks Jules Leroux; and he replies: 'The same as that of political science, namely to found *social science*.'[4]

With the Classical economists, economics was a science of the laws governing wealth. They described the phenomena of production, distribution, and consumption, and saw in man—Adam Smith's *homo œconomicus*—only a cogwheel in the machinery. But for the Romantics, 'the *human*

[1] *Premiers lundis*, ii. 92.   [2] Op. cit. ii. 93.
[3] *Le Producteur*, i. 400. Probably taken from Sismondi.
[4] *Revue Encyclopédique*, lvii. 540.

factor is that which dominates both economic and political factors. And the science which treats of it, or *social science* properly so called, likewise dominates both political and economic science.'[1] The same idea is better expressed by Jean Reynaud, writing in December 1831:

Political economy is not only a science of calculation. It is also a science of observation. It is impossible to arrive at results stamped with a true character of certitude and generality, when dealing with human questions, by considering men as mere mathematical abstractions, as agents or producers devoid of feeling and of passion; it would be strange ignorance or contempt of the dignity of man to think that one could so dispose of his personality.[2]

It is further evident that these encyclopedists aimed at replacing *a priori* speculation with the scientific study of social phenomena. Jules Leroux charges Smith and his disciples with 'breaking up reality into too many fragments'; separating the moral from the physical, they 'failed to take life into account', and hence economic facts 'seemed to them rigid by nature'. But the idea which dominates their work, namely that 'science is born of observation', is true, and preferable to the speculative theorization of Fourier and the Saint-Simonians.[3] Of significance in this connexion are a number of statistical studies made during this period of actual working-class living conditions.[4] But the Romantic genius was organic rather than

[1] *Revue Encyclopédique*, lviii (1833), 34. Italics of the original.

[2] 'Association lyonnaise', *Revue Encyclopédique*, lii. 765.

[3] *Revue Encyclopédique*, lviii. 35–36.

[4] Baron de Morogues, *De la misère des ouvriers* (Paris, 1832); Villeneuve-Bargemont, *Économie politique chrétienne, ou recherches sur la nature et les causes du paupérisme en France et en Europe* (Paris, 1834); A. Guépin and E. Bonamy, *Nantes au XIXᵉ siècle* (Nantes, P. Sebire, 1835); Villermé, *Tableau de l'état physique et moral des ouvriers employés dans les manufactures* (Paris, Renouard, 1840, 2 vols.); E. Buret, *De la misère des classes laborieuses en Angleterre et en France* (Paris,

analytic. Even in its most scientific form, Positivism, the fundamental tendency is to organize and unify, not patiently to observe.

The strength and weakness of the Romantic spirit lay in this organic instinct. It is triumphant in Wagnerian opera, in the Hegelian philosophy of history, and in great constructions like the *Port-Royal* of Sainte-Beuve and *La Comédie Humaine*. In economics and political science, the universal humanism of a Pecqueur marks a distinct advance upon the Classical economists.

Social economy as we understand it, says Pecqueur, is the science having as its object the most perfect organization, not only of a society, but of humanity at large; it is the art of world-wide association and solidarity.[1] . . . From our point of view economics embraces all the spiritual, as well as material, factors that can guarantee the ends of solidarity, equality, and liberty pursued by the human race. Thus, not only what is commonly called political economy but religion, justice, jurisprudence, the constitution of the authority of the family and of property, laws governing the inheritance or transmission of functions and the possession of instruments of production: in a word, the sum total of elements constitutive of societies will be an integral part of social and political economy, which accordingly is synonymous with social science.[2]

The reasons leading to the triumph of Marxism may be deduced from the same general cause. In the first place,

1845–6, 2 vols.); Adolphe Blanqui, *Les classes ouvrières en France en 1848* (Paris, 1849, 2 vols.); Agricol Perdiguier, 'Statistique du salaire des ouvriers' (in *Revue démocratique et sociale*, 1849); Hilde Rigaudias-Weiss, *Les enquêtes ouvrières en France entre 1830 et 1848* (Alcan, 1936, xii + 262 pp. Published by the Centre de Documentation sociale de l'École Normale Supérieure).

[1] Pecqueur defines *socialism* as 'the art of that science—applied social science'. *Le Salut du Peuple*, 10 December 1849, p. 10.

[2] *Théorie nouvelle d'économie sociale et politique*, Introduction, pp. i, ii.

Romanticism lacked a method to lay at the service of its idealism. In spite of its criticism of Classical economics it, too, relied almost exclusively on *a priori* reasoning. It is idle to look to works such as Pecqueur's *Théorie nouvelle* for an objective analysis of social realities. In the second place, religious enthusiasm led many of the Romantics into the errors denounced by Marx: the mysticism of the Saint-Simonians and of Fourier, or the Positivist worship of a 'Great Being', Humanity, of which it is impossible to tell whether it is a real existent or a general idea. Too often, a universe of moral relations co-ordinated together after the manner of the 'substantial forms' of the scholastics usurps the place of the real universe of social relationships, and, in Marx's phrase, 'alienates' man. It was left to the dialectical materialism of Marx to reverse an entire thought-process which came down to us from the Middle Ages.

Not all of Marx's predecessors, however, succumb in equal degree to the idealist temptation. The Encyclopedists in particular reject, as we have seen, the Utopianism of Fourier and Enfantin, and show a greater sense of political realism. 'It is not by freeing the passions from all control that we shall reach the goal of extending man's knowledge, his perfection of feeling and his mastery over nature', writes Jules Leroux in his article on 'Adam Smith', 'but by sacrifice, by manly virtue, by the path which the just and the strong have always followed and pointed out to others.'[1] By 1849 even the peace-loving Pecqueur had come to have doubts about progress by persuasion, and, enlightened by the experience of the February Revolution concerning the unwillingness of privileged classes to accept the loss of their privileges, began to speak of the 'inevitable and uniform solution of social problems by violence' and

[1] *Encyclopédie Nouvelle*, viii (1841), 195–6.

the 'eternal struggle between that which is and that which is becoming'.[1] Convinced that the sufferings of the people were 'the sole consequence of the mode of property-ownership obtaining today',[2] and with the strong sense peculiar to their age of the historical evolution of production processes and of institutions generally, the Leroux brothers form with Proudhon sober previsions of an era of 'mutual exchange' and, like him, call for new legislation founded on the socialization of the instruments of production.[3]

Much of the interest of Romantic literature for us today lies in its extraordinary blend of social realism and prophetic genius. Writers like George Sand and Victor Hugo saw the first great factories, the first railroads, take shape before their eyes; and they looked at these innovations, and at the social consequences of industrialism, with the simplicity and sincerity of which Michelet speaks so well: 'that divine innocence we sometimes glimpse in young things, only for a brief moment like a lightning-flash in the sky'.[4] It is the same childlike originality which Marx admires in the works of the ancients, and he adds, for him paradoxically, that 'the attraction of their art is indissolubly linked to the fact that the social conditions of which that art was born can never return'.[5] Michelet himself, in the Preface to his *Histoire du XIXe siècle*, illustrates this quality of Romantic literature perfectly. Looking at the Europe of 1800 he sees, in France, masses of men streaming towards the barracks; in England, masses streaming towards the factories. And his insight tells him it is the same thing: total mobilization, and tomorrow the threat

[1] 'Le Progrès par la Douleur', in *Le Salut du Peuple*, 10 April 1850.
[2] 'Échange', *Encyclopédie Nouvelle*, iv (1843), 455.
[3] *Encyclopédie Nouvelle*, viii (1841), 196–8.
[4] *Nos Fils.*
[5] *Über historischen Materialismus* (Berlin, 1930), ii. 83.

of total war. Machinery, he says, including administrative machinery, is giving men for the first time the means of joining forces without uniting their hearts, of living and working together without knowing one another: 'in this iron world whose motions are so precise, the one thing wanting is man.' And Michelet foresees the invention of a triumphant super-machine, an orthodox-thinking machine, which he calls *philosophie d'État*.[1] Not less interesting is his description of the psychological causes conducing to that end. 'The divorce is chiefly rooted in the absurd opposition drawn today, in the mechanistic age, between instinct and reflection. It lies in the contempt of the mind for those instinctive faculties which it mistakenly thinks it can dispense with.'[2] Sociologists today envy such writers what they call their freshness of perception and capacity for generalization. 'One may be taught how to pursue a course of questioning, how to map a neighbourhood, or how to tabulate and treat statistically the votes cast in an election', says Professor Redfield in a recent article on 'The Art of Social Science'; 'but to know how to do these things is not to be assured of meaningful conclusions.'[3] The author of a statistical study of working-class life in France during the Second Empire demonstrates how inferior, from the sociologist's point of view, is the testimony of the Realists.[4] A social psychologist devotes three volumes to Sainte-Beuve, considered as a *magnifique esprit sociologique*.[5] The literature of this great age, which not

[1] *Le Peuple* (second edition, Hachette-Paulin, 1846), 117–18.

[2] Op. cit. 168–72.

[3] *American Journal of Sociology*, November 1948, p. 186.

[4] G. Duveau, *La Vie ouvrière en France sous le Second Empire* (Gallimard, 1946).

[5] Maxime Leroy, *La Pensée de Sainte-Beuve* (Gallimard, 1940); *La Politique de Sainte-Beuve* (Gallimard, 1941); *La Vie de Sainte-Beuve* (Janin, 1947).

long ago it was commonplace to describe as extravagantly unreal, proves to have been not only true but prophetic.

Balzac is a realist, not because he went about fact-finding, like Zola, but—Baudelaire was right—because he had the Romantic vision. 'Society makes of man, according to the environment in which his activity is exercised, as many different species as exist in Zoology.'[1] Balzac was attentive to the emergence of new species: with one exception—the proletariat, *l'espèce ouvrière*, as Considerant calls it. He saw the first financial tycoons in modern history, and his *Maison Nucingen* anticipates *Das Capital*. His crooked politicians and shyster lawyers match the lithographs of Daumier. His gangsters and stool-pigeons are still with us. Balzac wrote the epic of the modern newspaper world. It is called *Illusions perdues*. He foresaw the advent of the twentieth-century bureaucrat, and describes him to the life in *Les Employés*. César Birotteau's assistants are archetypes of the department-store clerk. And no one has ever matched his travelling salesmen: 'les Voyageurs, ces intrépides affronteurs de négations'; the Illustrious Gaudissart is 'carved', as Raymond Mortimer says, 'on a gigantic scale, like the cherubs ten-foot-high in St. Peter's'.[2] 'Cet homme a tout vu, il sait tout, il connaît tout le monde.' The same might be said of Balzac. 'I have learned more from Balzac than from all the works of the historians, economists, and professional statisticians of the period taken together.' The author of this statement is Friedrich Engels.[3]

George Sand contributed an enthusiastic preface to the 1855 edition of the *Comédie Humaine*. To her one of

---

[1] *Avant-propos de la Comédie Humaine.*

[2] *Horizon*, December 1941.

[3] In *Les grands textes du marxisme: la littérature et l'art* (Éditions sociales internationales, 1936), 149.

Balzac's novels, the *Mémoires de deux jeunes mariées*, is dedicated; and in a letter to Madame Hanska he pays her this significant tribute: 'She has noble virtues, those which society takes the wrong way.'[1]

Romanticism is a school not only of social but of spiritual realism, without which no descriptions of human society are worth the paper they are printed on. The insight of its great writers into what they called the 'social destiny of man' is a function of the terms in which they appraised the relative importance of that destiny in relation to man's transcendent destiny as an individual. What future has a society which believes only in 'real' values, and does not admit that man lives in an eternal, as well as in a 'real' world? Such is the insistent question with which Balzac, the great realist, leaves us; it constitutes the underlying meaning of all his work. And there is, for the Romantics, no common measure between the fates of nations and the destiny of one solitary soul: in the former case we are dealing with problems, but in the case of the personality we face not problems but mystery beyond knowledge and beyond measure. 'Though it would be painful to us to see individual affections predominate over general', says the Saint-Simonian *Globe*, 'we intend that personality shall be respected, and not sacrificed to the other aspect of human life, for we know that mystery is the safeguard of the individual against society.'[2] And in some notes written for *Les Misérables* Hugo emphasizes the point when he writes:

Do away with poverty and destitution we can; but do away with suffering we can not. Suffering, we profoundly believe, is the law of this earth, until some new divine dispensation. . . . The quantity of fatality that depends on man is called Penury and can be abolished; the quantity of fatality that depends on

[1] *Lettres à l'étrangère*, i. 462.
[2] 'Du Mystère', *Globe*, 1 March 1832.

the unknown is called Sorrow and can only be contemplated in fear and trembling.[1]

The underlying motive of social romanticism is the libera-tion of the individual personality, and hence the moral and spiritual emancipation of mankind.

Freedom is not something that we have, or inherit, but something that we achieve by ceaseless effort every day. It is this effort that is dramatized in the life of the priest in *Jocelyn* (1836). Lamartine felt with Lamennais, on whose doctrines he largely drew, that social progress and a Christian spirit must go hand in hand. 'La charité', he wrote in 1834, 'c'est le socialisme.'[2] His humanitarian ideals as expressed in *La Politique rationnelle* (1831) re-produce in essence the programme of Lamennais's journal *L'Avenir* (1830-1); they include universal suffrage, free-dom of the press, freedom of conscience, and penal reform. His political activities have been sympathetically studied by Dr. Ethel Harris.[3] On his return from the East, where in 1832 he encountered the Saint-Simonians, he associated himself with Lamennais, Hugo, Ballanche, and Lecheva-lier (director of the *Revue du progrès social*) to organize in 1834 a *parti social*. Nothing came of the project, though it was revived in 1839 by Léon Brothier and Charles Le-monnier, two Saint-Simonians.[4] He announces his deci-sion in his 'Destinées de la poésie', published in May 1834. Lamartine's Defence of Poetry is at the same time an im-portant document of social history. Here is his analysis of the contemporary scene:

There are ages at which those institutions which represent

[1] Hugo, *Roman* (Ollendorff), iv. 554.
[2] *Voyage en Orient* (Hachette), ii. 477-8. This passage was written in July-Sept. 1834 (C. Maréchal, *Lamennais et Lamartine*, 292). Leroux's *De l'Individualisme et du Socialisme* had just appeared.
[3] *Lamartine et le peuple*.
[4] Weill, *L'École Saint-Simonienne*, 195-7.

the thought of mankind are organized and vital; society, at such periods, pursues the even tenour of her way. . . . But there are others when institutions, worn out by the lapse of time, are falling in ruins all around us, and when each of us must bring his stone and mortar to rebuild a shelter for humanity. It is my conviction that we stand at one of those great ages of social reconstruction and renewal. The question today is not merely whether the reins of power shall pass from royal hands to popular, whether the nobility, the priesthood or the middle class shall take control of the new governments, or whether we shall take the name of empires or republics: the question is deeper than that. What has to be decided is whether the ethical idea, the religious idea, the idea of evangelical charity, shall take the place of selfishness in politics. . . . The idea is ripe; the times are decisive; a small number of intelligences belonging to all the various denominations of political opinion bear the fertile thought in their heads and in their hearts. I am one of those who, without violence but with audacity and faith, mean at last to attempt to realize that ideal. . . .[1]

The distinction drawn in this passage between 'critical' and 'organic' periods shows the influence of the Saint-Simonian philosophy of history. Religiously, the thought recalls a page of the *Paroles d'un croyant*.[2] But when Lamartine writes 'La poésie, c'est l'idée; la politique, c'est le fait', we agree with M. Lanson that he borrows from *Stello* (1832), and would add that Vigny himself recalled Lamartine's 'Destinées de la poésie' when, a few weeks after its appearance, he wrote the preface to *Chatterton*.

Politically, Lamartine was the most active of all the Romantic writers. Having entered the Chamber of Deputies in 1833, he devoted himself with energy and conspicuous success to the interests of the working class. In a

[1] 'Des destinées de la poésie', in the Hachette (G.É.F.) edition of Lamartine's *Méditations poétiques*, ii. 421–2.
[2] See Maréchal, *Lamennais et Lamartine*, 290.

speech made exactly nine days before the first performance of *Chatterton*, on 3 February 1834, Lamartine warned the French Parliament of the danger of postponing measures of social reform, and said:

The proletarian question is one that will cause the most terrible explosion in present-day society, if society and government decline to fathom and resolve it.

The same year he took the floor on behalf of the unemployed, and proposed as a solution to the economic crisis through which the country was passing the reduction of customs tariffs and the colonization of Algeria. Lamartine, the great idealist, was unsparing of those politicians who 'lead the people, perverted by their example, to believe that there is no such thing as truth or falsehood, virtue or crime in politics, and that the world belongs to the shrewdest and the most audacious'. But great causes found in him an eloquent and effective champion; and his speeches in defence of the orphaned and the starving, against capital punishment, against slavery, and in support of the freedom of the press, were events in the political history of France in the first half of the nineteenth century, and were responsible for his very large popular following. When the Revolution of February 1848 broke out he became head of the Provisional Government. He proved to be a sagacious statesman, devoting himself to the reconciliation of class antagonisms and to a programme of moderate reform. His name is not only illustrious in the annals of French parliamentary life; it is, like Gladstone's in England, enshrined in the memory of the poor.

Jocelyn, *La Chute d'un ange*, and *La Marseillaise de la Paix* deserve to be ranked with *Les Pauvres Gens* and *Melancholia*. Lamartine projected a vast epic of humanity and its destinies, similar in scope to *La Légende des Siècles*; of this, *Jocelyn* and *La Chute d'un ange* are the *disjecta membra*. These poems are eloquent of his enthusiasms and admirations, and not less of the noble spirit in which he conceived his duty as a poet and as a statesman.

> Vous n'établirez pas ces séparations
> En races, en tribus, peuples ou nations;
> Et quand on vous dira: 'Cette race est barbare',
> 'Ce fleuve vous limite', ou 'Ce mont vous sépare',
> Dites: 'Le même Dieu nous voit et nous bénit,
> Le firmament nous couvre et le ciel nous unit!'
>
> Vous vous assisterez dans toutes vos misères,
> Vous serez l'un à l'autre enfants, pères et mères:
> Le fardeau de chacun sera celui de tous,
> La charité sera la justice entre vous;
> Le pardon, seul vengeur, remettra toute injure;
> La parole y sera serment sans qu'on la jure;
> Votre ombre ombragera le passant, votre pain
> Restera sur le seuil pour quiconque aura faim. . . .
>
> En retour du pardon que le ciel nous accorde
> Le plus beau don de l'homme est la miséricorde:
> Il la doit à son frère, à soi-même, à celui
> Qui seul a droit de juge et de vengeur sur lui;
> La vengeance ou l'erreur inventa le supplice:
> Ce monde vit de grâce, et non pas de justice.[1]

The socialism of Vigny reveals itself in his writings of the period 1831–9, notably his play *Chatterton* (1835). The poet was introduced to the ideology of the Saint-Simonians by Philippe Buchez, a physiologist and medical practitioner whom he met in 1828 and with whom he remained friendly for a number of years.[2] Founder of the earliest

---

[1] *La Chute d'un ange*, Canto viii.

[2] The chief works of Buchez are: *Introduction à la science de l'histoire* (1833); *Histoire parlementaire de la Révolution Française* (1834–8, 40

working-class co-operatives and first president of the Assemblée Nationale in 1848, Buchez exercised a marked influence on the French working-class movement through his journal *L'Atelier* (1840–50); in England, John Stuart Mill's advocacy of producer co-operatives and the programme of the Christian Socialists owe much to his writings.[1] The *Nouveau Christianisme*, to Buchez, was Saint-Simon's masterpiece; and he defined the significance of the Master's work as the integration of the eighteenth-century philosophical tradition with the idea of Christian charity.[2] After contributing some remarkable papers to *Le Producteur*, in December 1829 he parted with the Saint-Simonians, in whom he recognized the 'promoters of a new pantheism'[3] rather than disciples of Saint-Simon, and evolved a doctrine of his own with strong Catholic affinities. Expounded in 1830 to the Société des Amis du Peuple and in lectures given at his own home in the Rue des Quatre-Vents as the authentic 'Doctrine de Saint-Simon', it attracted many disciples. We have Balzac's testimony that Vigny frequently attended these meetings, for the poet figures in *Illusions perdues*, under the name of Daniel d'Arthez, as a member of the 'musico-philosophic and religious *cénacle* of the Rue des Quatre-Vents', as Balzac calls it, 'where serious young men assemble to discuss the general trend of humanity'. A genuinely Romantic spirit often inspired the lecturer.

Let no cold dialectician come vaunting to us the predominance of reason over passion, and telling us that feeling must be

vols., in collaboration with Roux-Lavergne); *Traité de philosophie au point de vue du catholicisme et du progrès* (1840); *Traité de politique et de science sociale* (1861).

[1] Mrs. Sidney Webb, *The Co-operative Movement in Great Britain*, Pt. I, chap. 5.
[2] *Introduction à la science de l'histoire*, 98.
[3] *Essai d'un traité complet de philosophie*, ii (1839), 323.

kept in check if the heart is to be healthy. No, to produce a moving harmony the most sensitive chords must be made to vibrate, and it is well to arouse the passions when one knows how to control them. Generous enterprises are not the product of hearts of ice. Arouse energetic indignation against vice, kindle an ardent love of virtue, make the heart of man beat vigorously if you wish to see him do great things. And in the light of that, gentlemen, you may appreciate at its proper value the kind of smugness with which our age seems to glorify in being eminently *positive*.[1]

There is evidence in the *Journal d'un poète* that in December 1829 Vigny contemplated taking an active part in the Saint-Simonian movement.[2] In this he was encouraged by his friend Sainte-Beuve, then writing to *Le Globe*. The poet had just produced at the Comédie-Française his version of *Othello*, and had been taken to task by his Saint-Simonian associates for so far neglecting 'the poet's mission' as to spend his talents on translation instead of 'studying the social needs of his time'.[3] 'Tragedy', wrote Dr. Boulland (a disciple of Buchez), 'classical or romantic, and whether Greek in subject-matter or medieval, Racinian or Shakespearean in form, tragedy is dead. It no longer corresponds to any need, and must disappear, yielding place to the *drame*, the *drame bourgeois* in nineteenth-century dress, mirroring the idleness and egoism of the age.' The same month, Sainte-Beuve addressed Vigny in verse, and urged him to turn his attention to the triumphs and sorrows of real life.

> La triste humanité monte à votre front d'ange . . .
> Vous abordez la vie et le monde et les drames,
> C'est bien; là sont des maux, mille dégoûts obscurs, . . .

[1] *L'Organisateur*, 25 December 1830.

[2] *Journal* (Scholartis Press), 24, 77, 88.

[3] Boulland, 'Le More de Venise', in *L'Organisateur*, 7 November 1829.

Mais aussi le triomphe immense, universel . . .
Méritez qu'on vous dise Apôtre en poésie.[1]

The poem *Paris*, which gives the Saint-Simonians a
conspicuous place in the contemporary intellectual firma-
ment, was written on 16 January 1831. It describes them,
in terms which perhaps intentionally recall Sainte-Beuve's
poem, labouring to construct a *Temple immense, universel*,

> Où l'homme n'offrira ni l'encens, ni le sel,
> Ni le sang, ni le pain, ni le vin, ni l'hostie,
> Mais son temps et sa vie en œuvre convertie,
> Mais son amour de tous, son abnégation
> De lui, de l'héritage et de la nation.

Reviewing this poem in its number of 9 May, the *Globe*
noted Vigny's sympathy with 'the sufferings of the most
numerous and impoverished classes' and commended his
dream of 'an association between all peoples, of which
Paris is to be the centre'. The reviewer's displeasure with
the sceptical note on which the poem ends did not prevent
him from recognizing in its author,

of all the poets of the Romantic School, the one who is en-
dowed with the most religious nature; . . . the artist most devoted to his art and the most capable of apprehending what
is incomplete, un-social and un-vital in the literary theories
of his friends, of grasping and bringing to fulfilment the full
value of a new and broader, loftier conception of literature.

The events leading to the schism of 1831 dampened
Vigny's Saint-Simonian ardour without lessening his interest in those rational ideas of the school which, as the *Globe*
correctly analysed, engaged his attention to the exclusion of its religious mysticism. The desire for independence of 'Associations' expressed in a famous chapter of
Stello (1832) was prompted by the policies of Enfantin,

[1] *Consolations*, xxvi.

which the *Journal* of the same year qualifies as 'une mascarade grotesque';[1] but when, two years later, he wrote *Chatterton*, the masterpiece of the Romantic social drama, the themes which crowded to his pen were almost always specifically Saint-Simonian.

In arranging for the stage the episode in *Stello* entitled 'Histoire de Kitty Bell', Vigny introduced some noteworthy changes. He brought in a new character in the person of the Quaker, who is represented as another of Kitty's lodgers, and Chatterton's confidant. Voltaire's Quaker in the *Lettres Philosophiques* partly served as a model; but Vigny's Quaker is also a doctor, and reminds us of the Docteur Noir of the novel and of the author's medical friends. Secondly, he gave much greater prominence to Chatterton himself, who in *Stello* appears only in two chapters (interview with the Lord Mayor and suicide). Again, John Bell, who in the novel is simply a saddler, became a great manufacturer; and a scene was introduced in which he receives a deputation of workmen from his factory.[2] In short, the characters of the novel became social symbols, and the play was a *drame de la pensée* written with the avowed intention of 'agitating a social question'.[3] John Bell represents the bourgeoisie, 'mistress of France', as we read in a passage of the *Journal d'un poète* which bears the stamp of Buchez.[4] Lord Beckford, who represents the State, is the mouthpiece of Benthamite ideas. Vigny draws on the *Doctrine de Saint-Simon, première année* for its critique of bourgeois utilitarianism and his own denunciation of 'toutes les iniquités et toutes les laideurs d'une société mal construite'.[5] Kitty Bell, symbol

[1] 'Ordonnance du Docteur Noir', *Stello* (Delagrave), 287–9; *Journal*, 216–17 (entry dated 1832).

[2] *Chatterton*, i. 2.

[3] *Dernière nuit de travail* and *Sur les Représentations du drame*.

[4] *Journal*, 236.   [5] *Chatterton*, ii. 5.

of divine Charity, finds none who understand her but the poet and her old friend the Quaker. The latter often speaks for the author, to whom Leroux's words pre-eminently apply:

A man of knowledge, the philosopher knows . . . that the forms of the present will vanish and that the future is about to appear. He must therefore prepare the way for the future.

A man of feeling, he is bound by sympathy to all that suffers, all that is oppressed in the world. . . .

An artist in the true sense of the word, how can he find Beauty on earth while the face of man is sullied by vice, darkened by ignorance, and disfigured by tears?[1]

The psychology of the poet, in *Stello* and in *Chatterton*, is typically Saint-Simonian; and the theme of the prophetic mission of poetry reproduces in part the argument of the *Doctrine*, in part the thesis of the youthful Auguste Comte on the 'spiritual authority', in some papers contributed by him to the Saint-Simonian *Producteur*.[2] When the poet cries: 'Hope has lost its anchor; Faith, its chalice; and Charity, its poor children'[3] he is embroidering Leroux's description of 'a society without faith, without hope, and without charity';[4] and in the same sentence he borrows again from that source when he writes: 'The Law is as godless and corrupt as a courtesan . . . , the Earth cries to the Poet for justice against those who restlessly search for its gold and say that man has no need of Heaven.'[5]

The inference to be drawn from these facts is not that

---

[1] *Réfutation de l'Éclectisme* (Gosselin, 1841), 251–2.

[2] On these points see my 'Alfred de Vigny and Positivism', *Romantic Review*, xxxv (1944), 288–98, and 'Vigny and the *Doctrine de Saint-Simon*', *Romantic Review*, xxxix (1948), 22–29.

[3] *Chatterton*, iii. 1.

[4] Pierre Leroux, *Aux Philosophes* (1831).

[5] 'Ils ont déclaré la loi athée de toute manière.' Leroux, *De l'Individualisme et du Socialisme*. This important essay appeared while the play was being written.

Vigny's writings show the mark of socialist propaganda, though the poet's 'partiality' was recognized by the *Revue Encyclopédique*, which in a review of the contemporary drama singled out *Chatterton* for special attention and detected in the voice of its author 'quelquesuns de ces pieux accents qui révèlent l'attente religieuse de Dieu'.[1] The point is that the poet was completely a citizen of his age. As Enfantin says in a letter of 25 October 1835, speaking of Romantic literature and its social context, 'we should not take too literally the forms which great poets give to their prophecies, but we should be careful to heed the god that moves within them'. The letter continues:

Thus I pay little attention to the *republicanism* of Chateaubriand, Lamennais, and Ballanche, or, to take that younger trinity, Sainte-Beuve, Reynaud, and Leroux. I do not accept the *forms* in which their warm imaginations prophesy to me. But I know what is at the centre of these great lives, and I know that religion, morality, and order are their Muses, and that for several years they have acquired a power of sympathy for the intense sufferings of the people; and the god within them persuades me that mankind is on the march towards an era of liberty, of honesty, and of truth. . . . Any government that despises art and has against it the voices of Lamartine, Berryer, Chateaubriand, Lamennais, Ballanche, Béranger, Sainte-Beuve, Reynaud, Leroux, Lerminier, Hugo, and Dumas, is bound to die of atrophy. No pensions or positions can assure it of the loyalty of such men, . . . who today, by an overwhelming majority, are mainly preoccupied with the improvement, moral, intellectual, and physical, of the state of the people.[2]

A recent manifesto which is at the same time a philosophy of literary history invites us to consider the position

[1] 'Du théâtre en 1834', *Revue Encyclopédique*, January–March 1835.
[2] *Œuvres de Saint-Simon et d'Enfantin*, xxx. 145–6.

of writers in the social situation of today. Literature, says Jean-Paul Sartre,[1] is perpetually the antagonist of conservative forces, and even in a classless society would continue to perform its essential part as the vehicle of autocriticism. When speaking of the eminent dignity of the personality as the supreme value of life, and of the mission of literature to combat orthodoxy, Sartre is in the tradition of Proudhon, Jean Reynaud, and Pierre Leroux. When he writes, 'Nous devons dans nos écrits militer en faveur de la liberté de la personne *et* de la révolution sociale', he reminds us of Vigny's motto: 'Seul et libre, accomplir sa mission.' It is evident that the existentialist movement in France today is assuming the character of a social idealism. To reintegrate literature with society by supporting and enlightening the just demands of the proletariat, such is the mission which Sartre assigns to contemporary writers under the name of 'engagement' or social responsibility. 'One does not write for slaves.'

Today no one doubts that literature has become something more than a mere pastime, or documentary record. The influence exercised by the writings of Sartre, of Camus, or of Malraux, is real and important. One should, however, be cautious in defining it. Increasingly, the influence of modern literature tends to be an intellectualist factor. Politically and socially it is less significant, in spite of the spread of popular education, than was a hundred years ago the influence of Victor Hugo; at least it is relatively much slower in reaching the masses. That the cultural lag has grown rather than decreased since the nineteenth century is hardly to be denied: though analphabetism has virtually disappeared illiteracy is still prevalent, and the important books of our time are read by only a limited public. It is to such representative modern arts as

[1] 'Qu'est-ce que la littérature?', in *Situations*, ii (Gallimard, 1948).

the motion-picture with its enormous popular audiences that it is logical to look today for the transmission of social ideas. Their possibilities as instruments in the service of democracy are only beginning to be realized.

Sartre admits that Hugo is perhaps the only great French author who was ever popular. Michelet, he says (and, he should add, Lamartine), had for some time a following; but the Romantic writers appear to him as 'les vaincus d'une révolution ratée', the Revolution of February 1848 having led only to the isolation of literature from society and the cult of art for art's sake, or the 'swindle' of so-called Realism. Sartre considers the modern divorce between writer and public 'a phenomenon without precedent in literary history', and, thinking of Flaubert and Baudelaire, traces its origins back to 1848. No one in the eighteen-thirties, according to him, conceived the possibility of an internal relation between the demands of the working-class on the one hand and the principles of the emergent new literature; only in the second half of the century did a virtual new public rise to encourage contradictions with bourgeois ideology. On this point Sartre's philosophy of literary history needs to be integrated with the history of the social movement. It was not after 1850 but in October 1830 that the journal Le Globe published the historic article 'Espoir et vœu du mouvement littéraire' in which Sainte-Beuve witnesses to the emergence of the virtual new public referred to by Sartre, and calls upon the Romantic writers to engage in 'the social movement which is gaining ground every day'.[1] The conception of a relation between the class-movement and the principles of a new literature appears contemporaneously in the Preface of Hernani. It is central to the aesthetics of Victor Hugo, and there is significance in the fact that the terms 'socialism' and

[1] Critiques et portraits littéraires, i. 255–61.

'symbolism' were both launched in France by a Romantic metaphysician. Sartre considers the socialism of Hugo, Michelet, and George Sand a 'by-product' of bourgeois idealism—like Marxism, and, Sartre would add, like Existentialism. But, as he appropriately remarks in his own defence, this does not imply that its fundamental insights were illusions of the bourgeois consciousness, or mythical representations of the human situation.

Literature gives us a special insight into intellectual and cultural antagonisms; and it is a real weakness of the materialist dialectic that it seems to underrate their importance, for their consequences are still with us. The revolt of the artistic intelligence against contemporary society is indeed a distinguishing feature of the modern age, and a sharp contrast to the attitude of the scientists, at least till the recent acquisition by scientists of an uneasy conscience. Modern psychology has given the phenomenon much study, and has supplied an explanation which for a time found wide acceptance, by defining poetic and artistic genius as a product of individual maladjustment. But when cases of maladjustment become as frequent as they have been in the history of recent art and literature, when they become so frequent as to constitute in a given age the rule rather than a number of picturesque exceptions, and when this rule establishes a contrast with the experience of other ages, the suspicion is not to be dismissed that the maladjustment may be seated in the social rather than in the individual consciousness. Wagner considers modern art as essentially revolutionary, springing from the conflict of the individual conscience with mass opinion; and he points to the remarkable contrast that it affords to the art of antiquity, which was an 'expression of all that was deepest and noblest in the popular conscience'. Carlyle and the French writers of a hundred years ago considered themselves a clergy. Wagner would go farther, and describe them as a clergy without a church. The search for a transcendence was a common concern of the age. Some turned to technical efficiency and industrial organization, others to scientific rigour and impartiality, others to the missionary function of art, to the dignity of labour, while yet others sought refuge in the ancient mercies of traditional faiths: in Stoicism, in the various sects of Christianity. The search went on, for the Romantic age was not romantic enough to satisfy the human need,

> The desire of the moth for the star,
> Of the night for the morrow. . . .

The poet Fernand Gregh wrote in 1913, apropos of Vigny's *Daphné*:

A secular ethics has yet to be constituted on solid and irrefutable foundations. We too, at this moment of world history which is perhaps symmetrical with the Roman decadence, . . . seem caught in the same dilemma as the Romans of the IVth century:—either faith, or anarchy. Without faith, morality crumbles, for we cannot, up to the present at least, conceive of an ethics apart from a mysticism. . . . But, on the other hand, it is difficult for the Europeans of today, as it was for the hellenized Romans of the time of Julian the Apostate, to have the faith in dogma of younger races.—Must then we too put our hopes in the coming of the Barbarians?

It was indeed strangely fitting that *Daphné*, which contains the fullest statement of Vigny's views on the subject of moral communion, should have appeared on the very eve of cataclysm. The critic goes on to express the wish that, despite appearances to the contrary, life may triumph over the destructive instinct.

Let us hope that we may succeed in building later on the purely humane system of ethics which today seems to us still impossible, or rather in creating, as Auguste Comte would have wished, a *mystique* of Life. This is a task to which philosophers, scientists, and artists should bend their energies without delay.

Clearly he was none too confident of such a solution: in fact he foresaw a new religion coming from Russia to conquer and revive Europe.[1] Since 1913, while our best minds have been more than ever preoccupied with moral problems those problems seem farther than ever from receiving a solution, and the outlook of the early socialists has become increasingly foreign to us. But in the political aspect of the problem we have seen authoritative and violent solutions applied which in the more civilized atmosphere of 1913 would have appeared incredible.

Comte's 'control of opinion' has become a reality. Today it is a function of the State, using as its instruments the educational system and media of mass information. This has led in some countries to a dissolution of democracy.

The seeds of reaction lie deep in the Romantic age. Romanticism, of course, is a European movement; and it is necessary to remember the three phases in its history. The earliest period is liberal and revolutionary. It is the period of the *Lyrical Ballads*. The youthful Wordsworth sympathized with the democratic ideals of the French Revolution, while Coleridge and Southey dreamt of establishing Pantisocracy on the banks of the Susquehanna. The next period is pre-eminently the period of the German Romantic movement, and coincides with the Napoleonic Wars. In all countries the writers of this period went over to the side of reaction. Wordsworth became the 'Lost Leader' of a new generation. Scott's novels fell in with the trend to nationalism, but also contributed much to the beginnings of the third 'great Romantic communion',[2]

[1] Preface to *Daphné* (Delagrave, 1913), pp. xxiv–xxvi.
[2] Fernand Baldensperger, 'La grande communion romantique de 1827: sous le signe de Walter Scott', *RLC.*, vii (1927), 47–86.

that in which France joined. And the most important reactionary thinkers of the century are not German, but French.

In the works of Joseph de Maistre and the Vicomte de Bonald[1] fear of the Revolution led to fantastic conclusions. Convinced of the sinfulness of man, these writers called for a return to absolutism, with the Pope as the final arbiter and the executioner for his henchman. In his *Mont des Oliviers* Vigny stigmatizes De Maistre as one of the 'false prophets' who betrayed the Man of Calvary. A chapter of *Stello* is devoted to a criticism of his doctrine of expiatory suffering,[2] while in *Servitude et grandeur militaires* the soldier-poet repudiates the dogma of war as divinely ordained.

Malgré les paroles d'un sophiste que j'ai combattu ailleurs, il n'est point vrai que . . . la guerre soit *divine*; il n'est point vrai que *la terre soit avide de sang*. La guerre est maudite de Dieu et des hommes mêmes qui la font et qui ont d'elle une secrète horreur.[3]

Indirectly, however, Vigny owed to De Maistre more than he perhaps realized, for it was from *Du Pape* that both Comte and Saint-Simon, the poet's direct sources, drew

[1] Joseph de Maistre, *Considérations sur la France* (1796); *Du Pape* (1819); *Soirées de Saint-Pétersbourg* (1821). Vicomte de Bonald, *Théorie du pouvoir politique et religieux* (1796). On these writers see H. J. Laski, *Authority in the Modern State* (Oxford, 1919).

[2] *Stello*, chap. xxxii (Delagrave, 209–10).

[3] *Servitude et grandeur militaires* (Conard), 71. There is an essay on 'Joseph de Maistre et A. de Vigny' in F. Baldensperger's *Alfred de Vigny, contribution à sa biographie intellectuelle* (Hachette, 1912), 49–69. I think this essay exaggerates Vigny's debt to De Maistre. M. Baldensperger denies that in *Stello* the Docteur Noir is speaking for the author; but the reference in *Servitude et grandeur* to 'un sophiste que j'ai combattu ailleurs' clearly shows that he is. Further, M. Baldensperger does not recognize the Catholic philosopher in *Le Mont des Oliviers*; but the doctrine of *raison d'état* ('il est permis pour tous de tuer l'innocent') is as characteristic of De Maistre as of Machiavelli.

important elements of their doctrine of the 'spiritual authority' and their admiration of the political system of the Middle Ages.[1]

The chief difference between the German reactionaries and the French is that the Romantic writers in Germany do not distinguish the idea of the State from the idea of Society. Their conception of the State is to a large extent a protest against the 'isolation of private interest and private property'[2] under the system of liberal bourgeois economics; there is hardly an argument of twentieth-century fascism which they do not bring to bear against the liberal ideas of their time.[3] Professor Lovejoy has pointed out how the political conceptions of contemporary fascism originate in aesthetic or metaphysical ideas of the Romantic period in Germany.[4] He shows how a particular group of those ideas—the totalitarian idea of transcendental idealism and of the Romantic aesthetic; the dynamic idea culminating in Nietzsche's Will to Power; and the equally Romantic cult of diversity (*Eigentümlichkeit*), transferred from the individual to a race of *Herrenvolk*—'have produced in our time a sort of joint-effect, which is at least an essential and conspicuous part of the monstrous scene presented by Germany and by Europe today'. It is the more to be regretted that he has not amplified this statement by showing how so grotesque a travesty of idealism was able to be made by an intelligent race; to that question the answer must be sought in the irrational but none the less real motives of maddening fear,

---

[1] Lévy-Bruhl, *La Philosophie d'Auguste Comte*, 345–6.

[2] Adam Müller, *Elemente der Staatskunst*, i. 291.

[3] The critical argument of national socialism is well stated by Werner Sombart in his *Deutscher Sozialismus*, translated under the title *A New Social Philosophy* (Princeton University Press, 1937). It is the constructive argument which is reactionary.

[4] A. O. Lovejoy, 'The Meaning of Romanticism for the Historian of Ideas', *JHI*, ii (1941), 257–78.

anxiety, and desperation. Of these we have spoken in the
context of a hundred years ago. They were even more acute
in the Germany of the nineteen-twenties and nineteen-
thirties. It was these dark forces which raised the ghost
of the 'Third Reich' from musty folios of the twelfth
century.[1] An interesting case has been made for the influence upon the Romantic movement of mystical thought.[2]
The influence of the irrational on politics is as great today
as it was a hundred years ago. It thrives on the mass-
insanity induced by fear, anxiety, and despair.

To turn from these political theories to the revolutionary
ideas of the French Romantics is to emerge from the
twilight of unreason into the brightness of day. Maurras
and Lasserre were entirely right in considering the revolutionary *mystique* as essentially Romantic, and entirely
wrong in describing it as of German origin.[3] Leroux, for
example, whose works offer the best summation of French
political Romanticism, never wavers in his adhesion to the
revolutionary concept. He never fails to rate the values of
personality above the claims of the State, nor does he
cease to exalt the dignity of the common man. That
government should become 'a giant hydra embracing in
its toils the whole of society', and the individual be nothing
more than its 'humble, submissive servant',[4] this is not for

---

[1] The Cistercian abbot Joachim of Floris (*c.* 1145–1202) prophe-
sied that a *Drittes Reich* or Reign of the Holy Ghost would dawn in
the year 1260, when an *ordo iustorum* would arise and found upon
a spiritual interpretation of Scripture the *evangelium aeternum*. De
Maistre took up this prophecy.

[2] A. Viatte, *Les Sources occultes du Romantisme: illuminisme, théo-
sophie* (Champion, 1928, 2 vols.); *Victor Hugo et les illuminés de son
temps* (Montreal, 1942).

[3] P. Lasserre, *Le Romantisme français, essai sur la révolution dans
les sentiments et les idées du XIXᵉ siècle* (Paris, 1907). Charles Maurras,
Romantisme et Révolution (Paris, 1925).

[4] 'Cours d'économie politique', *Revue Encyclopédique*, October
1833.

him the goal of universal history, the cause for which 'Socrates and Jesus divinely died'.[1] Some of his utterances foreshadow the totalitarian state, as when he writes:

The citizen becomes a State servant. He is regimented, he has an official doctrine to believe in, and the Inquisition on his doorstep. Man is no longer a free, spontaneous being, but an instrument obeying involuntarily and making mechanical responses to the action of society.

Then follows an admirable expression of the democratic idea:

Every man reflects within himself the whole of society. Every man is in a certain way the manifestation of his age, his nation, and his generation; every man is humanity; every man is a sovereignty; every man is a law, for whom laws are made, and against whom no law can prevail. . . . The perfection of society is in ratio to the liberty of all and of each.[2]

For the will to power, French Romanticism substitutes a will to justice. Racialism it replaces with the doctrine of internationalism. 'The whole body of civilization . . . has always been the land of the poet's higher allegiance. . . . That country knows no other frontier than the dark line where ignorance and servitude begin.'[3] Instead of totalitarianism it offers the doctrine of liberty, 'man's sovereignty over himself'.[4] These are the great principles of 1789.

The assertion of the inviolability of the personality is of special moment to us today, living as we do at a crisis of the concept of freedom. It has been well expressed in a recent work of the Communist poet Aragon.[5] It is of course

[1] De l'Égalité, 270.
[2] 'Cours d'économie politique', Revue Encyclopédique, October 1833.
[3] Preface to Les Burgraves. Théâtre (Ollendorff), iii. 496–7.
[4] Les Misérables, v. i. 5. Roman (Ollendorff), vi. 25.
[5] Louis Aragon, Le Crève-cœur (Horizon–France Libre, 1942).

an assertion of the value of freedom, and therefore of law. It is the principle of modern law that any freedom which does not violate the freedom of others is inviolate and inalienable. The reason for this is not always well understood. We often talk as if freedom of speech and of the press, freedom from want and oppression, were the crux of the matter; yet these freedoms are rightly prized only as means to the larger freedom. Deprived of the opportunity of making his choice of all possible thoughts, including wrong thoughts, man loses the capacity of thought and of will. Freedom implies the possibility of error. That is the high price we must pay for wisdom. To think that others can pay that price for us and that men can be regulated into perfection is in essence a blasphemous arrogation to human agencies of divine omniscience, or papal infallibility. The preposterousness of the authoritarian assumption is apparent if we suppose that at the place where we are now situated one group of gentlemen is omniscient, while at a point thirty miles away their omniscience ceases and another group of gentlemen begins to be omniscient. *Plaisante omniscience qu'une frontière borne!*

Authoritarianism is rejected not merely because it is irrational and oppressive, but because it is immoral. This brings us to the aspect of political and social Romanticism which is perhaps least understood today. There is a tendency today to place an emphasis which the Romantics would have considered typically bourgeois upon social security and better living-conditions as ends. Not that they disagreed as to the desirability of these things, but they would certainly not have considered welfare measures an adequate solution to the problems of modern society. They did not admit that the fuller and more abundant life we seek could be bought at the cost of a number of budgetary arrangements. The concern of the socialists of 1830 is with the 'construction of a new social order'.[1] Nothing short of total regeneration could in their view suffice. And on this essential point the identity of views between Marx and the Romantics is complete.

Political and administrative standards, according to Marx, can never be at a higher level than the economic structure and cultural development of a society;[2] in a society whose ethical purposes do not rise above them, only a progressive decline of morale is to be expected. The rise of the welfare-state appeared to many great writers of the past century as a menace of authoritarianism. Napoleon III tried to ingratiate himself with the masses by means of a programme of social legislation including free medicine for the needy, the establishment of a scheme of old-age pensions, workmen's compensation, and health insurance. As a result he swept all before him at successive plebiscites, thus initiating the technique used by the twentieth-century dictators. But he did not succeed in corrupting the democratic leaders of 1848. Victor Hugo, with unquenchable faith and unbending hostility to the Second Empire, went on championing what to others seemed lost causes. The first to raise his voice against the triumph of an immoral politics, he wrote in his magnificent *Châtiments* the most meaningful of books for us today.

> J'accepte l'âpre exil, n'eût-il ni fin ni terme,
> Sans chercher à savoir et sans considérer
> Si quelqu'un a plié qu'on aurait cru plus ferme,
> Et si plusieurs s'en vont qui devraient demeurer.

---

[1] 'La *construction* d'un NOUVEL ORDRE SOCIAL': *Doctrine de Saint-Simon* (Rivière), 151 *et passim*. Italics and capitals of the original. The term is also used by Fourier.

[2] *Ausgewählte Schriften* (Moscow, 1934), ii. 571 ff.

> Si l'on n'est plus que mille, eh bien, j'en suis! Si même
> Ils ne sont plus que cent, je brave encor Sylla;
> S'il en demeure dix, je serai le dixième;
> Et s'il n'en reste qu'un, je serai celui-là![1]

The pledge thus given to the cause of freedom he kept to the letter, returning from nineteen years of self-imposed exile only when the tyrant was overthrown. This was in 1870. The fatal sequence had begun which led to 1914 and 1939. Counter-revolution was on the march.

In the France of 1944 Victor Hugo, according to an underground newspaper, was the French author most often read and quoted, and the forces of resistance regarded him as the 'poète épique du peuple libre promu à la conscience et à la parole'. 'He reminds us of the great revulsion of the French people against an earlier form of fascism.'[2] It is because his life and work are the incarnation of the democratic *Idée* that Hugo seems to us the most important and most representative nineteenth-century writer. Time after time he sought to arouse the conscience of mankind against tyrants.

> Ils ont des surnoms, Juste, Auguste, Grand, Petit,
> Bien-Aimé, Sage, et tous ont beaucoup d'appétit.
> Qui sont-ils? Ils sont ceux qui nous mangent. La vie
> Des hommes, notre vie à tous, leur est servie.
> Ils nous mangent. Quel est leur droit? Le droit divin....
>
> Est-ce qu'ils ont pour voix la foudre? Ils ont la voix
> Que vous avez. Sont-ils malades? Quelquefois.
> Sont-ils forts? Comme vous. Beaux? Comme vous. Leur
>   âme?
> Vous ressemble. Et de qui sont-ils nés? D'une femme.

---

[1] 'Ultima Verba', *Les Châtiments*, vii. 17.

[2] Reproduced in the *Cahiers français*, a publication of the French Committee for National Liberation, no. 54 (April 1944), p. 29.

Ils ont, pour vous dompter et vous accabler tous,
Des châteaux, des donjons. Bâtis par qui? Par vous. . . .[1]

We inherited from the nineteenth century the dilemma
of freedom and order which its ruling class was too busy
to solve. It has involved us in two world wars, in which
the issues of responsible government and of popular sovereignty underwent trial by ordeal. Counter-revolution
under new names sought the classical way out—Caesarism.
Peoples rallied behind it, driven by the primitive instinct
to escape from chaos, and repudiating ties of solidarity
with a democracy which seemed to have to offer the world
only a variety of materialism whose values were infantile
and whose benefits they were denied. War, famine, and
suffering brought us to realize that there are in life values
more urgent than prosperity, or comfort, or novelty. War
in fact supplied what in peace was missing—a common
cause; for six years it created a community transcending
all frontiers—the Red Cross, tragic and final evidence of
civilization's deep need. It is a need of inner harmony
and peace. But peace should not be considered as a mere
absence of foreign war. Spinoza defines it in positive and
universal terms as 'a virtue, springing from courage and
strength of character'.[2] Its establishment can never be the
work of politicians alone. It can only come from the active
vigilance of an enlightened public opinion; labour leaders,
newspaper-men, writers, philosophers, artists, clergy, and
teachers have the key responsibilities: political possibilities
are determined by their action, or their failure. Should we
despair of our ability to exercise in peace the virtue of
solidarity which war has taught us to recognize? It is the
key to that 'new harmony', as Fourier and Robert Owen

[1] 'Les Mangeurs', *Légende des Siècles* (Cercle des Tyrans).
[2] 'Pax enim non belli privatio, sed virtus est, quae ex animi forti-
tudine oritur.' *Tractatus theologico-politicus*, v. 4.

called it, towards which men have been feeling their way
for more than a hundred years.

> Le jour n'est pas levé. — Nous en sommes encore
> Au premier rayon blanc qui précède l'aurore
> Et dessine la terre aux bords de l'horizon.

A BIBLIOGRAPHY OF
FRENCH SOCIALISM
FROM SAINT-SIMON
TO PROUDHON

PART I

GENERAL

ANDLER, CHARLES PHILIPPE THÉODORE. *Le Manifeste communiste de Karl Marx et F. Engels*. Introduction historique et commentaire. Paris, Rieder, 1922. 209 pp.

Prehistory and sources of the *Communist Manifesto*. The fact which emerges from Andler's detailed analysis is that the influence of French ideas on Marx and Engels was very considerable, especially the thought of Pecqueur and of Bazard (inaccurate on Pecqueur). He does not consider Leroux, whose critique of contemporary society often invites a comparison.

Review: In *RScPol*, xlv (1922), 632.

BOUGLÉ, CÉLESTIN CHARLES ALFRED. *Chez les prophètes socialistes*. Paris, Alcan, 1918. 246 pp.

On the descent of French socialism from Saint-Simonism. M. Bouglé presents a case for considering the French socialist tradition independently of Marxism. He examines the tenets of Marx in the light of modern sociology.

Review: A. Ouy in *RIS*, xxvii (1919), 542–3.

BOUGLÉ, CÉLESTIN CHARLES ALFRED. 'Le Romantisme social', in *Le Romantisme et les Lettres*. Paris, Montaigne, 1929, pp. 267–81. First published in *Annales de l'Université de Paris*, Sept. 1928.

M. Bouglé shows that the conventional picture of the Romantic writer as a 'jeune homme désespéré qui pleure sur un roc solitaire' does not correspond to the facts.

BOUGLÉ, CÉLESTIN CHARLES ALFRED. *Socialismes français. Du 'Socialisme utopique' à la 'Démocratie industrielle'*. First ed. 1932; 2nd ed., Paris, Colin, 1933. viii+200 pp.

In this valuable little book the author (Professor of Social Economy at the Sorbonne and Directeur du Centre de Documentation sociale de l'École Normale Supérieure) summarized the results of a life-time of research. It contains an excellent analysis of the three principal French socialist doctrines (Saint-Simonism, Fourierism, and Proudhonism) together with a 'balance-sheet' of their still vital elements. A lengthy introduction deals with the eighteenth century and the Revolutionary period. The Bibliography (pp. 191–200) is exceptionally complete.

Reviews: In *RIS*, xl (1932), 454; H. Gouhier in *NRF*, xxxix (1932), 305–8; H. Sée in *Rhist*, clxx (1932), 137–8; G. Bourgin in *RC*, xcix (1932), 366–7; M. A. Bloch in *Rph* (1935), i. 275–6.

BOURGIN, GEORGES and HUBERT. *Le Socialisme français de 1789 à 1848*. Paris, Hachette, 1912. viii+111 pp.

A brief outline of the subject, illustrated by a series of representative texts. The authors are at pains to establish the revolutionary origins of French socialism, a debatable point.

Reviews: A. Biovis in *RC*, lxxiv (1912), 279; R. G. in *RC*, lxxvii (1914), 315.

BUIS, LUCIEN. *Les Théories sociales de George Sand*. Paris, Pedone, 1910. 207 pp.

A juridical study of George Sand's novels and their background. Buis concludes that the novelist underwent three main influences: those of the Saint-Simonian school, of Leroux, and of Louis Blanc (in chronological order). He excludes Fourier, injudiciously. Chapter iv contains a good summary of her 'communism'.

CASSAGNE, ALBERT. *La Théorie de l'art pour l'art en France chez les derniers romantiques et les premiers réalistes*. Paris, Hachette, 1906. ix+487 pp. Thèse de l'Université de Paris.

Part I, chap. ii, pt. 2: social literature under the July Monarchy.

CHARLES-BRUN, JEAN. *Le Roman social en France au xixᵉ siècle*. Paris, Giard-Brière ('Études économiques et sociales'), 1910. iii+363 pp.

While the bulk of this study concerns the novel of manners of the second half of the century, two chapters (pp. 74–127) deal with the Romantic novel (George Sand, Eugène Sue, and Victor Hugo).

CHARLÉTY, SÉBASTIEN. 'La Restauration des Bourbons', in Ernest Lavisse, *Histoire de la France contemporaine depuis la Révolution jusqu'à la Paix de 1919*, vol. iv. Paris, Hachette, 1921.

Book II, chap. 3 contains a parallel study of the rise of socialism and of the advent of romanticism; Book III, chap. 3, a precise account of living-conditions, based on a wealth of statistical material.

CHARLÉTY, SÉBASTIEN. 'La Monarchie de Juillet', in Ernest Lavisse, *Histoire de la France contemporaine depuis la Révolution jusqu'à la Paix de 1919*, vol. v. Paris, Hachette, 1921.

Book I, chaps. 1 and 3 continue the account of social doctrines begun in the previous volume, linking them with contemporary literature. Book II, chap. 4 deals with economic conditions. Invaluable both for literary history and for the history of ideas.

Reviews: H. Buffenoir in *RC*, lxxxviii (1921), 344–6; in *RScPol*, xlv (1922), 623–4; R. Guyot in *Rhist*, cxliii (1923), 65–6.

DOLLÉANS, ÉDOUARD. *Histoire du mouvement ouvrier*. 2 vols. Paris, Colin, 1936–7, third ed., Paris, Colin, 1947–8. 2 vols.

Dealing mainly with the July Monarchy, the first volume of this monumental work gives a graphic account of the beginnings of the working-class movement in France and Great Britain. Dolléans does not exaggerate the importance of economic factors in social history; the value of his work lies in his intimate knowledge of the Chartists and their French contemporaries, and in his profound humanism.

Reviews: L. Cheronnet in *NL*, 5 December 1936; G. Bourgin in *Rhist*, 180 (1937), 136–8; P. Laroque in *Sciences Politiques*, lii (1937), 68–71, liv (1939), 210–13; G. Friedmann in *Annales d'histoire sociale*, i (1939), 430–1.

EVANS, DAVID OWEN. 'L'Évolution du théâtre social en France de 1750 à 1850', *RSH*, xxxix (1925), 51–63.

Continuity from Nivelle de la Chaussée to Augier and Dumas fils.

EVANS, DAVID OWEN. *Le Roman social sous la Monarchie de Juillet*. Paris, Presses Universitaires, 1930. 167 pp.

With a bibliography (pp. 21–34) of social, political, and apostolic novels of the period.

Reviews: In *TLS*, 14 May 1931; D. Mornet in *RHL*, xliii (1936), 445–6; J. G. Tricot in *Revue bibliographique et critique*, no. 31–2 (May 1936).

FLOTTES, PIERRE. *La Pensée politique et sociale d'Alfred de Vigny*. Paris, Belles-Lettres, 1927. xvi+360 pp. Publications de la Faculté des Lettres de Strasbourg.

Flottes studies the relation of Vigny's thought to the contemporary doctrines of Joseph de Maistre, de Tocqueville, Saint-Simon, Buchez, Ballanche, &c., using unpublished material drawn from the poet's memoirs. He sums up Vigny as a 'penseur social . . . comme malgré lui', but his study of influences neglects the economic and social environment.

Reviews: P. Martino in *RC*, xciv (1927), 419-20; in *RLC*, vii (1927), 362-3; E. Estève in *RHL*, xxxv (1928), 276-8.

FOURNIÈRE, EUGÈNE. *Le Règne de Louis-Philippe*. Paris, Rouff, s.d. (1906). 583 pp. Vol. viii of the *Histoire socialiste (1789–1900)*, ed. by Jean Jaurès.

Statistics on the condition of industry, on pauperism, mortality-rates, &c.

Review: A. Mathiez in *RC*, lxxii (1906), 454-7.

FOURNIÈRE, EUGÈNE. *Les Théories socialistes au xixe siècle, de Babeuf à Proudhon*. Paris, Alcan, 1904. xxi+415 pp.

History of ideas: the origin and evolution of the concepts of modern socialism in the first half of the nineteenth century. Fournière sums up the tenets of the leading schools of socialist thought on such points as feminism, the State, property, capital, &c. The French authors represented are mainly Babeuf, Saint-Simon, Bazard, Enfantin, Pecqueur, Vidal, Fourier, Proudhon, Cabet, Leroux, and Louis Blanc.

Reviews: G. L. Duprat in *RIS*, xii (1904), 850; L. Gérard-Varet in *Rph* (1905), ii. 210-15.

GIDE, CHARLES, and RIST, CHARLES. *Histoire des doctrines économiques depuis les Physiocrates jusqu'à nos jours*. Paris, Larose et Tenin, 1909. xix+766 pp. Seventh revised ed., Paris, Sirey, 1947. xx+901 pp.

The chapters on Saint-Simonism (Book II, chap. 2), Fourierism (Book II, chap. 3, pt. ii), and Proudhonism (Book II, chap. 5) bring out clearly analogies and contrasts between these systems and State socialism or Marxism. A standard text-book on the history of economic thought (Engl. trans., Heath, s.d. xxiii+672 pp.), one of its merits is that it is eminently readable. To say that the physiocrats were the founders of social science is perhaps an exaggeration.

Reviews: R. Worms in *RIS*, xxi (1913), 750-1; M. Aucuy in *RHES*, viii (1920), 109-10.

GIRARD, HENRI. 'La Pensée religieuse des romantiques. A propos d'un livre récent', *RHL*, xxi (1925), 79-97.

Replying to Viatte's *Le Catholicisme chez les Romantiques* (Paris, Boccard, 1922), Girard points to the indebtedness of Lamartine, Vigny, and Hugo to Lamennais, Leroux, and the Saint-Simonians.

GROS, J. M. *Le Mouvement littéraire socialiste depuis 1830*. Paris, Michel, s.d. (1904). 323 pp.

Written at second hahd and full of inaccuracies, this work, part of which (pp. 1–115) deals with the doctrines of the July Monarchy and with the social novel, drama, and *chanson*, nevertheless supplies a general perspective which is useful.

GUILLEMIN, HENRI. *Lamartine et la question sociale*. Genève, La Palatine, 1946. i+219 pp.

Using unpublished documents from the Saint-Point archives, the exegetist of *Jocelyn* presents Lamartine as pre-eminently a lucid personality with a strong civic sense, all his life pursuing the plan of action outlined in his *Politique rationnelle*: not social, but liberal, democracy. In Guillemin's conception of lucidity there is a suggestion of Machiavellianism.

GUYON, BERNARD. *La Pensée politique et sociale de Balzac*. Paris, Colin, 1947 (1948). xvii+829 pp.

The formation of Balzac's social and political thought from 1820 to 1834, and his evolution from liberalism to legitimism. Light on his relation to the Saint-Simonian movement (pp. 315–29, 345–49). Guyon brings his study to an end with the *Médecin de campagne* on the doubtful grounds that political conditions had become 'stabilized' in 1833, and that Balzac's later works contain nothing new (the views on property in *Les Paysans* are not considered).
Review: J. Pommier in *RHL*, l (1950), 330–3.

HALÉVY, ÉLIE. *Histoire du socialisme européen*. Paris, Gallimard, 1948. 367 pp.

Edited by the Société des Amis d'Élie Halévy, this book represents lectures given at the École des Sciences Politiques from 1898 to 1936. The first two chapters deal with British and French socialism. Halévy considers *Das Capital* as 'not a *point de départ* but a *point d'arrivée*'.
Review: R. Pagosse in *RSoc*, xxxi (1949), 375.

HARRIS, ETHEL. *Lamartine et le peuple*. Paris, Gamber, 1932. 549 pp.

A noteworthy biographical study of Lamartine the idealist and humanitarian, written from first-hand sources consulted at Saint-Point. Dr. Harris emphasizes Lamartine's sense of mission, arising from direct familiarity with the lives of the working class. She is inclined to underrate doctrinal influences, and her Bibliography (pp. 449–75) is somewhat deficient in respect of them.
Review: P. Martino in *RC*, xcix (1932), 471–2.

HUNT, HERBERT J. *The Epic in Nineteenth Century France. A Study in Heroic and Humanitarian Poetry.* Oxford, Blackwell, 1941. xiii+446 pp.

No history of Romanticism would be complete without a record of its audacious failures. Rediscovering many forgotten authors and obscure works, Dr. Hunt reveals the little-suspected importance of the epic strain in nineteenth-century poetry; his descriptive account, accompanied by bibliography and index, provides a useful guide amid the *disjecta membra* of this grand Romantic project. The most noteworthy single chapter is that devoted to Ballanche (chap. v, pp. 74–100).

Reviews: In *TLS*, 23 August 1941; J. A. Bédé in *RR*, xxxiv (1943), 274–9; A. Schaffer in *MLN*, lviii (1943), 298–300; J. Voisine in *RHL*, xlix (1949), 280.

HUNT, HERBERT J. 'L'Impulsion socialiste dans la pensée politique de Victor Hugo', *RHL*, xl (1933), 209–23.

Answering Professor Schinz's *L'Unité dans la carrière politique de Victor Hugo*, Dr. Hunt rightly emphasizes the republicanism of Hugo's writings after 1851, and finds the unity of his political thought in his humanitarian socialism.

HUNT, HERBERT J. *Le Socialisme et le Romantisme en France: étude de la presse socialiste de 1830 à 1848.* Oxford, Clarendon Press, 1935. x+399 pp.

Dr. Hunt examines the press of the Saint-Simonian and Fourierist schools, and presents a well-organized account of their judgement of Romantic literature. The conclusion drawn, that there was a close link between Romantic literature and the movement of ideas, may be considered demonstrated. The Bibliography is a trustworthy guide to the literary field but needs to be supplemented for the history of doctrines.

Reviews: M. Halbwachs in *RC*, cii (1935), 247–8; in *TLS* (1936), 670; K. Wais in *Archiv*, clxix (1936), 152; G. Bourgin in *Rhist*, clxxvii (1936), 167–8; F. Lefèvre in *NL*, 19 Sept. 1936; M. E. I. Robertson in *MLR*, xxxii (1937), 113–14.

ISAMBERT, GASTON. *Les Idées socialistes en France de 1815 à 1848; le Socialisme fondé sur la fraternité et l'union des classes.* Paris, Alcan, 1905. 426 pp. (Bibliothèque de philosophie contemporaine).

Laski considered this the best work on the subject (*Communism*, p. 252). Isambert gives an excellent historical and comparative account of all the doctrines anterior to 1848, together with an appreciation of each. In his emphasis on ethnical factors he tends to overlook the importance of the historical process, especially the growth of the spirit of class warfare, in all countries.

Reviews: A. Landry in *RIS*, xii (1905), 667–8; E. Fournière in *RSoc*, xlii (1905), 248–9; J. Delvaille in *Rph* (1905), ii. 426–8; É. Halévy in *Annales de l'École Libre des Sciences politiques*, xxi (1906), 407–9.

KARÉNINE, WLADIMIR (Madame Komarow). *George Sand, sa vie et ses œuvres*. Paris, 1899–1926. 4 vols. Vols. i, ii, Plon-Nourrit, 1899. Vol. iii, Plon-Nourrit, 1912. Vol. iv, Ollendorff, 1926.

The works of George Sand are a confluence of many streams of thought, and in view of her influence in Russia it is appropriate that the most precise and best-informed study of her life and work should have been written by a Russian lady. Madame K. combines sympathy for her subject with the utmost discernment in evaluating the various influences which the novelist assimilated. These four volumes, with a useful index, are a storehouse of information on French socialism.

Review: W. Haape in *ZFSL*, xxxvii (1910), ii. 59; xli (1913), ii. 61–75.

LEBLOND, MARIUS-ARY. 'George Sand et la Démocratie', *RPar*, xi (1904), 75–102.

George Sand's life and service to democracy, especially from 1841 onwards. The chief influences noted are those of Madame d'Agoult and Pierre Leroux.

LEBLOND, MARIUS-ARY. 'Notes sur George Sand socialiste', *RSoc*, xl (1904), 28–49, 174–90.

The 'unity' of her 'intellectual and social life' is explained in terms of Rousseau's doctrine of equality.

LE BRETON, ANDRÉ. 'La Pitié sociale dans le roman. L'auteur des *Misérables* et l'auteur de *Résurrection*', *RDM*, lxxii (1902), 889–915.

Social compunction in Hugo's novel; its influence on Tolstoy.

LEROY, MAXIME. *Histoire des idées sociales en France*. Vol. i: De Montesquieu à Robespierre. Paris, Gallimard, 1946. 385 pp.

M. Leroy makes a strong case for the continuity of social thinking from the eighteenth century to the twentieth. He considers that his predecessor Lichtenberger (*vid. inf.*) was mistaken in his subject, being too much influenced by Marxist definitions. And it is for *le social*, i.e. signs of concern about institutions, not *le socialisme*, that M. Leroy looks in the eighteenth century, with striking results.

Reviews: É. Dolléans in *RHES*, xxvi (1947), 69–78; P. Kahn in *CIS*, iii (1947), 179–81; L. Febvre in *Annales*, iv (1949), 375.

LEROY, MAXIME. *La Politique de Sainte-Beuve*. Paris, Gallimard, 1941. 289 pp.

Sainte-Beuve impresses the social historian as a *magnifique esprit sociologique*. That his criticism has as its focus all the social phenomena of his generation, and belongs as much to the history of social ideas as to the history of literature: such is the thesis which M. Leroy victoriously defends. The chapter 'Sainte-Beuve Saint-Simonien' (pp. 29–114) outlines the *Port-Royal* of the nineteenth century which remains to be written.

Review: É. Dolléans in *RHES*, xxvi (1947), 72.

LEROY, MAXIME. *Les Précurseurs français du socialisme, de Condorcet à Proudhon*. Paris, Temps présent, 1948. 447 pp.

A selection of annotated texts, with biographies. The introduction deals with the continuity and the diversity of socialist thought.

Review: Dom Nicolas Perrier in *Témoignages*, xxiii (1949), 462.

LICHTENBERGER, ANDRÉ. *Le Socialisme au XVIIIe siècle, étude sur les idées socialistes dans les écrivains français du XVIIIe siècle avant la Révolution*. Paris, Alcan, 1895. viii+470 pp. Thèse de doctorat ès lettres (Sorbonne).

A well-documented though tendentious account of Rousseau, Montesquieu, Diderot, Voltaire, and of the lesser eighteenth-century precursors (Saint-Pierre, Meslier, Mercier, Restif de la Bretonne, Mably, Linguet, &c.). The 'socialism' of the age is the protest of the *philosophes* against inequality.

Reviews: H. Monin in *RC*, xl (1895), 187–9; E. Fournière in *RSoc*, xxii (1895), 502–3; in *RIS*, iv (1896), 680; in *Rph* (1896), ii. 310–11.

LOUIS, PAUL. *Louis Blanc, Vidal, Pecqueur, Cabet*. Paris, Librairie de l'Humanité, 1922. 72 pp.

Bio-bibliographical notices of each of these writers are followed by selected pages from their works.

Review: R. Picard in *RHES*, xi (1923), 128.

LOUIS, PAUL. *Cent cinquante ans de pensée socialiste: Babeuf, Saint-Simon, Fourier, Owen, Considerant, Blanqui, Pecqueur, Leroux, Cabet, Louis Blanc, Vidal, Proudhon, Marx, Engels, Lassalle, Benoît Malon, Lafargue, Guesde, Jaurès, Plekhanov,*

Lénine. Marcel Rivière (Bibliothèque des Sciences Politiques et Sociales), 1947. 263 pp. 1st ed., Rivière, 1938–9, 2 vols.

An anthology, with brief biographies and summaries of each of the doctrines. Paul Louis emphasizes the importance of the early nineteenth century.

LOUVANCOUR, HENRI. *De Henri de Saint-Simon à Charles Fourier. Étude sur le socialisme romantique français de 1830.* Chartres, Durand, 1913. 452 pp. Thèse pour le doctorat en droit (Paris).

A study of the relations between the two schools. Louvancour makes an instructive comparison of the doctrines and gives a first-hand account of the chief schismatics who in 1832 went over to Fourier, and of their subsequent activities. There is an important chapter on polemics.

MARSAN, JULES. *La Bataille romantique*. Vol. ii. Paris, Hachette, 1924.

Chap. iii, 'Du roman lyrique au roman social', an outline of the development of the social novel from George Sand's early works to *Les Misérables*, is one of the best-documented studies of the novel of this period.

MOREAU, PIERRE. 'Le Romantisme', in J. Calvet, *Histoire de la littérature française*, vol. viii. Paris, Gigord, 1932. 546 pp.

Pp. 247–373: 'Le Romantisme social et religieux', with a bibliography.

PICARD, ROGER. *Le Romantisme social*. New York, Brentano, 1944. 437 pp.

This splendid general study of the inter-relations of Romanticism and of Socialism falls into two parallel divisions: the social ideas of the Romantic writers, and the Romanticism of the contemporary socialists. The author, a distinguished economist and historian, has written a guide that was greatly needed, though it presents no new material and attempts no demonstration of influences.

POISSON, JACQUES. *Le Romantisme social de Lamennais, essai sur la métaphysique des deux sociétés (1833–1854)*. Vrin, 1932. 472 pp.

A thorough and weighty study. Poisson has read some little-known works of Lamennais. He studies his theory of the two societies, temporal and spiritual. He considers Lamennais as the social metaphysician, and not as the sociologist. A very interesting chapter is devoted to the ternary rhythm of the metaphysical systems of the Romantic age; another, to the social mission of art.

PUECH, JULES L. *La Tradition socialiste en France et la Société des Nations*. Paris, Rivière, 1921. x+228 pp. Preface by Charles Gide.

The internationalism of the French socialists. The point on which they divided was whether the World Federation which they all wished to see established should or should not be a super-State.

Reviews: H. Faron in *RIS*, xxx (1922), 395; H. Puget in *RScPol*, xlv (1922), 316–17; G. Richard in *Rph*, xcvi (1923), 154–5.

PUECH, JULES L. *La Vie et l'œuvre deFlora Tristan*. Paris, Rivière, 1925. iii+514 pp.

Flora Tristan, novelist and militant feminist who claimed descent from Montezuma and was Gauguin's grandmother, is an important link between Romanticism and the socialist movement. Her romantic life is the subject of the first 300 pages of this book, her socialism, of the remainder.

Reviews: A. Ouy in *RIS*, xxxv (1927), 79–81; Th. Ruyssen in *Rph*, ciii (1927), 155–6.

RAGON, MICHEL. *Les Écrivains du peuple, essai d'histoire de ce courant littéraire, depuis avant 1848*. Paris, Vigneau, 1947. 300 pp.

This work recognizes the pioneering done by Michelet and by the proletarian writers of the Romantic period who first created a popular literature: Agricol Perdiguier, Magu, &c. A fault of the book is, as Professor Dolléans has pointed out, its injustice to George Sand.

ROUGET, MARIE THÉRÈSE. *George Sand 'socialiste'*. Lyons, Bosc, 1931. 222 pp. Diss. (Doctorat d'Université, Dijon).

The thesis is that George Sand owes more to Rousseau than to contemporary socialists. Mlle Rouget goes much farther than M.-A. Leblond, and almost denies her socialism. A wider reading of the socialists of the period would have necessitated a modification of her views. George Sand's influence upon Russian novelists and the French social novel of the late- nineteenth century has been well described.

Review: P. Trahard in *RHL*, xxxix (1932), 607.

SCHINZ, ALBERT. 'L'Unité dans la carrière politique de Victor Hugo', *RHL*, xxxix (1932), 15–44.

Schinz finds the unifying principle in the alleged fact that all his life Hugo was an anti-democrat. See H. J. Hunt in *RHL*, xl (1933), 209–23 for an opposite statement.

sée, henri. *La Vie économique de la France sous la Monarchie censitaire (1815–1848)*. Paris, Alcan, 1927. 191 pp.

Chap. ii: 'L'évolution industrielle de la France; les progrès du machinisme et de la concentration', and chap. iii: 'La condition de la classe ouvrière', provide the best outline of the background of economic and social realities.

Review: H. Hauser in *RC*, xciv (1927), 443–5, takes Sée to task for neglecting literary documentation.

seillière, ernest antoine aimé léon, Baron. *George Sand mystique de la passion, de la politique et de l'art*. Paris, Alcan, 1920. xiii+456 pp.

Seillière considers George Sand's writings an example of that 'irrational imperialism' which, according to him, is the religion of contemporary Europe. Book II (pp. 145–250) deals with her social mysticism and its sources, viz. Lamennais and Leroux. The statements that Leroux was a disciple of Hegel and read him in the original, that he shared Enfantin's 'mysticisme passionnel', and that he was an apostle of metempsychosis, argue unfamiliarity with his writings.

Review: L. R. in *RC*, lxxxviii (1921), 408–10.

soltau, roger. *French Political Thought in the Nineteenth Century*. London, Benn, 1931. xxxi+500 pp.

Pp. 129–64: 'Towards a Socialist Society'.

van der linden, jacques p. *Alphonse Esquiros: de la Bohème romantique à la République sociale*. Paris, Nizet, 1948. 237 pp.

The works of the minor Romantics offer interesting junctions of literary, political, and social Romanticism. An early admirer of Hugo's dramas and a member of the Bohemian *cénacles*, Esquiros came under the influence of Lamennais, Louis Blanc, Pierre Leroux, and Jean Reynaud; M. Van der Linden thinks that from him Baudelaire derived the themes of several poems in his *Fleurs du mal* together with important elements of his general aesthetics. A well-documented thesis.

vianey, joseph. (Editor) Victor Hugo, *Les Contemplations*. Paris, Hachette, 1922. 3 vols. (GÉF series).

Vol. I, Introduction, pp. lxviii–lxxiii: an important though inaccurate account of socialist influences.

viatte, auguste. *Victor Hugo et les illuminés de son temps*. Montreal, L'Arbre, 1942. 284 pp.

Part of this learned study treats of the contemporary socialists, especially the disciples of Fourier.

PART II

SAINT-SIMONISM

ŒUVRES DE SAINT-SIMON ET D'ENFANTIN. Paris, Dentu (and E. Leroux), 1865–78. 47 vols.

Prepared by Enfantin's executors and edited by Laurent (de l'Ardèche), aided by Fournel, Guéroult, and others. Vols. i–xiii, Notices historiques (lives of Saint-Simon and Enfantin), with *Table générale* in vol. xiii.

CLAUDE HENRI DE ROUVROY, COMTE DE SAINT-SIMON (1760–1825)

ŒUVRES DE SAINT-SIMON. In *Œuvres de Saint-Simon et d'Enfantin*, vols. xviii–xxiii, xxxvii–xl. 1868–75.

ŒUVRES CHOISIES DU COMTE HENRI DE SAINT-SIMON CONTENANT SES PRINCIPAUX OUVRAGES SCIENTIFIQUES, MORAUX, POLITIQUES ET RELIGIEUX. Brussels, Castel, 1859. 3 vols.

Edited by Charles Lemonnier.

Lettres d'un habitant de Genève à ses contemporains (Paris, 1802), *réimprimées conformément à l'édition originale*. Edited by Alfred Pereire. Paris, Alcan, 1925. lx+90 pp.

Saint-Simon's first work re-edited, together with some unpublished *Lettres aux Européens* and an *Essai sur l'organisation sociale*, also hitherto unpublished.
Review: in *RScPol*, xlix (1926), 159.

(With Augustin Thierry, 'son élève'). *De la réorganisation de la société européenne, ou de la nécessité et des moyens de rassembler les peuples de l'Europe en un seul corps politique, en conservant à chacun son indépendance nationale* (Paris, Delaunay, 1814). Edited with introduction and notes by Alfred Pereire. Paris, Presses Françaises (Bibliothèque Romantique), 1925. xlvi+100 pp.

Review: R. Picard in *RHES*, xiv (1926), 139.

Du Système industriel. Paris, Renouard, 1821–2. 3 vols.

Catéchisme des Industriels. Paris, Sétier, 1823–4. 3 vols.

The third *cahier* signed by Auguste Comte.

*Nouveau Christianisme: dialogue entre un conservateur et un nova-
teur.* Paris, Boulanger, 1825. viii+91 pp.

The last work published in Saint-Simon's lifetime.

BARTHÉLEMY PROSPER ENFANTIN (1796–1864)

ŒUVRES D'ENFANTIN. In *Œuvres de Saint-Simon et d'Enfantin,*
vols. xiv–xvii, xxiv–xxxvi, xli–xlii, xlvi. 1868–74, 1878.

Editor (with H. Carnot, H. Fournel, Charles Duveyrier).
Doctrine de Saint-Simon. Exposition. Première année 1829 (Paris,
Bureau de l'*Organisateur*, 1830; also in *Œuvres*, vol. xli). Intro-
duction and notes by C. Bouglé and É. Halévy. Paris, Marcel
Rivière, 1924. 504 pp.

The text is mainly by Bazard.

Reviews: H. Mazel in *MF*, clxxvi (1924), 197–8; R. Picard in
RHES, xii (1924), 434–5; J. Prévost in *NRF*, xxv (1925), 360–2; in
RScPol, xlix (1926), 143.

*Enfantin. Textes choisis précédés d'une introduction par Sébastien
Charléty.* Paris, Alcan (Collection des Réformateurs sociaux),
1931. 108 pp.

Reviews: R. Durand in *RC*, xcviii (1931), 371–2; in *Rph*, cxiv (1932),
310–11.

SAINT-AMAND BAZARD (1791–1832)

Editor (with H. Carnot). *Doctrine de Saint-Simon. Exposition.
Seconde année 1829–30.* Paris, Bureau de l'*Organisateur* et du
Globe, 1830. 172 pp. Also in *Œuvres*, vol. xlii.

The text mainly by Enfantin.

Prédications (1831–32). Edited by Émile Barrault. Paris, Johanneau, 1832. 2 vols.

Also in *Œuvres*, vols. xliii–xlv.

*Religion Saint-Simonienne. Procès en la Cour d'assises de la Seine
les 27 et 28 août 1832.* Paris, Librairie Saint-Simonienne, 1832.
405 pp.

Also in *Œuvres*, vol. xlvii.

FOURNEL, HENRI. *Bibliographie Saint-Simonienne. De 1802 au 31
décembre 1832.* Paris, Johanneau, 1833. 130 pp.

The Bibliothèque Nationale possesses an interleaved copy with
numerous manuscript additions (Rés. p. Z 1217 (1)).

ALLEMAGNE, HENRY RENÉ D'. *Les Saint-Simoniens* (*1827–37*). Paris, Gründ, 1930. 453 pp. Preface by Sébastien Charléty.

Reproduces a wealth of first-hand documents on the Saint-Simonian movement and its picturesque personalities, drawn from the Archives at the Bibliothèque de l'Arsenal and from those of the Pereire family. The same author has published an inventory of the Saint-Simonian collection at the Arsenal. *Catalogue général des manuscrits des bibliothèques publiques de France*, xliii. 1–115.

Reviews: S. Charléty in *Rhist*, clxv (1930), 180; R. Picard in *RHES*, xviii (1930), 396.

ANON. 'A Pioneer of Socialism', *TLS*, 28 May 1925, pp. 357–8.

A well-informed short account of the life and chief works of Saint-Simon.

BERNSTEIN, SAMUEL. 'Saint-Simon's Philosophy of History', *Science and Society*, xii (1948), 82–96.

Dialectical elements in Saint-Simon's view of history.

BONNEFON, PAUL. 'Maxime du Camp et les Saint-Simoniens', *RHL*, xvii (1910), 709–35.

Maxime du Camp's Saint-Simonian fervour of the period 1851–8, when he opened the columns of the *Revue de Paris* to Flaubert, Bouilhet, Fromentin, and the Saint-Simonians, as related in his correspondence with Enfantin. The author is greatly mistaken in thinking that this doctrine which 'séduisit tant de généreuses intelligences' had no influence on art or literature.

BOUGLÉ, CÉLESTIN CHARLES ALFRED. *L'Œuvre d'Henri de Saint-Simon*. Paris, Alcan, 1925. xxxii + 264 pp.

Selected texts, with introduction by Prof. Bouglé and bibliographical notice by Alfred Pereire.

Reviews: F. Bertrand in *RC*, xcii (1925), 395–6; R. Picard in *RHES*, xiii (1925), 216; in *Rph*, ciii (1927), 312.

BRUNET, GEORGES. *Le Mysticisme social de Saint-Simon*. Paris, Presses françaises (Études romantiques), 1925. 125 pp.

Applying the Bergsonian method to the study of the thought of Saint-Simon, Brunet discovers at its core the idea of social salvation. He attaches greater weight to the *Nouveau Christianisme* than do other authorities.

Review: R. Picard in *RHES*, xiii (1925), 217–18.

BUTLER, ELIZA MARIAN. *The Saint-Simonian Religion in Germany. A Study of the Young German Movement.* Cambridge University Press, 1926. xiii+446 pp.

The *Doctrine* (1830) and its influence on Heine, Laube, Gutzkow, Mundt, and Wienbarg, with special reference to the 'rehabilitation of the flesh'. The criticism has been made that Miss Butler ignores other sources of feminist theory, specifically the ideas of Friedrich Schlegel and of Herder, but she has written a most readable and informative book, with a useful bibliography including books, pamphlets, and articles (1830–5).

Reviews: W. Kurrelmeyer in *MLN*, xlii (1927), 482–4; L. A. Willoughby in *MLR*, xxiii (1928), 102; Ch. Andler in *RC*, xcv (1928), 512–14; R. Palgen in *RLC*, ix (1929), 196–201.

CASTELLA, GASTON. *Buchez.* Paris, Bloud, 1911. 64 pp.

Reproduces 'Buchez historien, sa théorie du progrès dans la philosophie de l'histoire' (in *Études historiques de Fribourg*, vol. v, 1909), a study of the *Introduction à la science de l'histoire* (1833), preceded by a brief Life.

CHARLÉTY, SÉBASTIEN. *Essai sur l'histoire du Saint-Simonisme.* Paris, Hachette, 1896. 498 pp. Later eds. entitled *Histoire du Saint-Simonisme (1825–64).* Paris, Hachette, 1896. 506 pp. Paris, Hartmann, 1931. 386 pp.

The standard work on the subject. Like all Charléty's works it is distinguished by a vivid style and keen psychological insight. The latest edition brings the bibliography up to date. It is the best bibliography of Saint-Simonism (pp. 365–79).

Reviews: A. Lichtenberger in *RC*, xlii (1896), 377–9; P. Malapert in *Rph* (1896), ii. 309–10; A. Bochard in *RIS*, v (1897), 75–77; F. Ponteil in *Rhist*, clxviii (1931), 405–6; R. Durand in *RC*, xcviii (1931), 367–71; R. Picard in *RHES*, xix (1931), 468–9.

CUVILLIER, ARMAND. *P. J. B. Buchez et les origines du socialisme chrétien.* Paris, Presses Universitaires, 1948. 83 pp.

This little book supplies a real need, for the personality and thought of Buchez have been too much neglected. Cuvillier speaks informatively of the career of Buchez as historian, journalist, and organizer of working-class co-operatives. His literary relations deserve further study.

CUVILLIER, ARMAND. 'Un Schisme Saint-Simonien: les origines de l'école buchézienne', *Revue du Mois*, 10 June 1920, pp. 494–532.

Based on manuscript material drawn from the Archives Saint-

Simoniennes and from the Buchez collection at the Bibliothèque de la Ville de Paris.

DUMAS, GEORGES. *Psychologie de deux Messies positivistes: Saint-Simon et Auguste Comte*. Paris, Alcan, 1905. 316 pp.

Dumas's Messianic Saint-Simon is a contrast to Maxime Leroy's *philosophe*. The author, an experimental psychologist, proposes to show the indebtedness of Comte to Saint-Simon, both for his philosophic ideas and for his mysticism. On this see the next item.

Reviews: E. Fournière in *RSoc*, xlii (1905), 247–8; G. R. d'Allonnes in *Rph* (1906), i. 336–40; R. Worms in *RIS*, xv (1907), 62–3.

DUMAS, GEORGES. 'Saint-Simon père du Positivisme', *Rph*, lvii (1904), 136–57, 262–87.

On this hotly debated point cf. P. Janet, 'La Philosophie d'Auguste Comte', *RDM*, lxxxii (1887), 593–629; L. Lévy-Bruhl, *La Philosophie d'Auguste Comte*, Paris, Alcan (1900), pp. 345–6; Émile Durkheim, 'Saint-Simon fondateur du positivisme et de la sociologie', *Rph* (1925), 321–41; H. Gouhier, *infra*.

DURKHEIM, ÉMILE. *Le Socialisme, sa définition, ses débuts. La doctrine Saint-Simonienne*. Paris, Alcan, 1928. xi+352 pp.

Posthumously published by Marcel Mauss, this work is now of interest for Durkheim rather than for Saint-Simonism. It is based on a course given at Bordeaux in 1895–6 on the History of Socialism. Certain chapters were published separately.

Reviews: H. Mazel in *MF*, ccvi (1928), 162–3; É. Halévy in *RScPol*, lii (1929), 471; R. Picard in *RHES*, xvi (1928), 265–7; H. Sée in *Rhist*, clx (1929), 163–4.

EICHTHAL, EUGÈNE D'. 'Carlyle et le Saint-Simonisme. Lettres à G. d'Eichthal', *Rhist*, lxxxii (1903), 292–307.

Eugène d'Eichthal has also published *John Stuart Mill, Correspondance inédite avec Gustave d'Eichthal* (Paris, Alcan, 1898).

EVANS, DAVID OWEN. 'Alfred de Vigny and Positivism', *RR*, xxxv (1944), 288–98.

Chatterton and *La Maison du berger*.

EVANS, DAVID OWEN. 'Vigny and the *Doctrine de Saint-Simon*', *RR*, xxxix (1948), 22–29.

Textual evidences of the influence of the 1830 *Doctrine*.

FAGUET, ÉMILE. 'Le comte de Saint-Simon', *RDM*, cxxiii (1894), 856–81. Also in *Politiques et moralistes du xixe siècle* (Paris, Lecène-Oudin, 1891), vol. ii.

Faguet, no impartial critic of socialist writers, calls Saint-Simon 'un fou très intelligent' and studies his 'idée fixe'.

Review: J. Capperon in *Annales de l'École libre des Sciences politiques*, vi (1891), 387–9.

GOUHIER, HENRI. *La Jeunesse d'Auguste Comte et la formation du Positivisme.* Vol. ii: *Saint-Simon jusqu'à la Restauration.* Paris, Vrin, 1936. 350 pp.

Vol. ii of this study of the origins of Positivism constitutes a close examination of the life and works of Saint-Simon, with whom Comte was intimately associated for six years. Gouhier denies that Comte borrowed from Saint-Simon. 'Il s'agit d'idées courantes liées aux derniers développements de la science et de l'histoire morale de la Révolution.' The point remains contentious.

Review: H. Sée in *Rhist*, clxxii (1933), 352; A. George in *NL*, 10 Oct. 1936; P. Masson-Oursel in *MF*, cclxxxii (1938), 360–1.

GROSSMAN, HENRYK. 'The Evolutionist Revolt against Classical Economics. I—In France: Condorcet, Saint-Simon, Simonde de Sismondi', *JPE*, li (1943), 381–96.

The influence of the Saint-Simonian philosophy of history upon economic thinking.

JANET, PAUL. 'Le Fondateur du socialisme moderne. Saint-Simon. L'École Saint-Simonienne', *RDM*, 15 April 1876, pp. 758–86; 1 Oct. 1876, pp. 587–618.

Published on the completion of the *Œuvres* (1865–76), these articles provide an excellent critical synopsis but are in other respects outdated.

LENOIR, RAYMOND. 'Henri de Saint-Simon', *Rph*, c (1925), 179–222.

Saint-Simon is presented as the *grand seigneur* and has the honours of a philosophical disquisition.

LEROY, MAXIME. *Le Socialisme des producteurs: Henri de Saint-Simon.* Paris, Rivière, 1924. xix+195 pp.

Saint-Simon as a Cartesian rather than a Utopian. Leroy places him much above his predecessors Rousseau and Babeuf, or his followers Fourier and Marx, because of his conception of government which is entirely rational.

Reviews: G. Bourgin in *Rhist*, cxlvii (1924), 279–80; R. Picard in *RHES*, xii (1924), 447–8.

LEROY, MAXIME. *La Vie véritable du comte Henri de Saint-Simon.* Paris, Grasset, 1925. 336 pp. (Cahiers verts.)

Seeking the historical personality behind the legendary figure, M. Leroy emphasizes Saint-Simon's eighteenth-century background and represents him as more the *philosophe* than the mystic. New evidence is brought to light suggesting that his four years' service in the American Revolutionary War probably had much to do with the turn of his thoughts.

Reviews: R. Picard in *RHES*, xiii (1925), 217; in *RScPol*, xlix (1926), 143.

LODEWIJK DE LIEFDE, CAREL. *Le Saint-Simonisme dans la poésie française entre 1825 et 1865.* Haarlem, Amicitia, 1927. 192 pp. Diss., Amsterdam.

This study is, as Dr. H. J. Hunt says, a courageous contribution to knowledge of social poetry by minor authors contemporaneous with the Romantic movement. But it is deficient in background: Lamartine and Leconte de Lisle are mistaken for Saint-Simonians.

Reviews: P. Martino in *RHL*, xxxvi (1929), 602–3; J. Giraud in *RHL*, xxxviii (1931), 125–6.

MURPHY, ELLA M. 'Carlyle and the Saint-Simonians', *SP*, xxxiii (1936), 93–118.

Miss Murphy thinks that Carlyle's debt to Saint-Simonism has been exaggerated, pointing to *Signs of the Times* (1829) as evidence of his early preoccupation with social problems.

PASQUIER, ALBERT. 'Saint-Simon et les problèmes du temps présent, essai d'anticipation posthume', *RHES*, xxvii (1948), 26–46.

The twentieth-century evolution of the capitalist system and the Russian model of a directed economy judged from a Saint-Simonian standpoint.

PEREIRE, ALFRED. *Autour de Saint-Simon.* Paris, Champion, 1912. xii+239 pp.

Contains much material of interest in connexion with Saint-Simon's collaborators, especially Auguste Comte. Many pages are devoted to the views on credit and banking of the Pereire brothers.

Review: G. Bourgin in *Rhist*, cx (1912), 403.

PICARD, ROGER. 'Un Saint-Simonien démocrate: le docteur Ange Guépin', *RHES*, xiii (1925), 456–94.

Guépin's *communalisme*, a democratic mystique akin to the thought of Reynaud and of Leroux. Remarkably well documented.

POLINGER, ELLIOTT H. 'Saint-Simon, the Utopian Precursor of the League of Nations', *JHI*, iv (1943), 475–83.

The *actualité* of Saint-Simon's political ideas.

SÉCHÉ, LÉON. *Le Cénacle de Joseph Delorme (1827–30).* Paris, Mercure de France, 1912. 2 vols.

Vol. i, chap. 9, on Sainte-Beuve and Saint-Simonism.

SÉCHÉ, LÉON. *Sainte-Beuve.* Paris, Mercure de France, 1904. 2 vols.

Vol. i, chap. 2, on the same. Consult also G. Michaut, *Sainte-Beuve avant les Lundis* (Fribourg, 1903), chap. viii.

SÉE, HENRI. *La notion de classes sociales chez les Saint-Simoniens.* Paris, Rivière, 1926. 6 pp.

The chief novelty of the Saint-Simonian doctrine is its critique of the theory of property.

SHINE, HILL. *Carlyle and the Saint-Simonians. The Concept of Historical Periodicity.* Baltimore, Johns Hopkins Press, 1941. xiii + 191 pp.

Shine examines *Sartor Resartus, The French Revolution, Lectures on the History of Literature,* and *Heroes,* showing how the Saint-Simonian philosophy of history assisted Carlyle in systematizing his own ideas. He promises a later treatment of the influence of the social ideas of the Saint-Simonians. It is to be hoped that before making it he will supplement his first-hand readings of Saint-Simonian literature with a reading of some of the more important studies of the movement which have appeared in the course of the past fifty years.
Review: Emery Neff in *MLN*, lviii (1943), 241.

SPÜHLER, WILLY. *Der Saint-Simonismus. Lehre und Leben von Saint-Amand Bazard.* Zürich, Girsberger, 1926. xii + 173 pp. Zürcher Volkswirtschaftliche Forschungen, vii. Diss., Zürich.

Regarding the *Doctrine* as mainly the work of Bazard, the author subjects it to a treatment less impersonal than has usually been given it. He rightly emphasizes the collectivism of Bazard's doctrine; but few will agree with him in his appreciation of Comte as a mere pupil

of Saint-Simon, or of Enfantin as a degenerate. He contributes an appendix on the relation of the *Doctrine* to German socialism, and a remarkably interesting chapter on Saint-Simonism in economic life.
Review: E. L. in *RHES*, xiv (1926), 398–9.

THIBERT, MARGUERITE. *Le Rôle social de l'art d'après les Saint-Simoniens.* Paris, Rivière, 1926. 75 pp. Thèse supplémentaire (Paris).

Based on a reading of Barrault's *Aux Artistes* (1830) and other Saint-Simonian writings, this study shows that the evolution of Saint-Simonism in a collectivist sense after 1830 was accompanied by an increasing sympathy for Romantic literature. Madame T. examines (*a*) the Saint-Simonian aesthetic; (*b*) the literary and artistic work of various adherents. She omits mention of what is perhaps the most characteristic literary work of the school: Duveyrier's drama *L'Ingénieur* (1836). The whole subject awaits fuller treatment.

WEILL, GEORGES. *Un Précurseur du socialisme. Saint-Simon et son œuvre.* Paris, Perrin, 1894. x+247 pp.

The opening to the public of the Saint-Simonian archives in 1894 led to the writing of several studies which are still standard references. This is one of the earliest. It is a biography of Saint-Simon followed by an analysis of the origins of his socialism as it appears in his many works. One chapter (chap. xi) deals with his influence on Comte. There is also a noteworthy chapter on the economic condition of France and on economic theory at the close of the Empire. A digest, by the author, was published in *RIS* (1893), i. 517–27.
Reviews: P. Lagarde in *RSoc*, xx (1894), 122; in *RHL*, i (1894), 393; G. Monod in *Rhist*, lv (1894), 385; L. G. Varet in *Rph* (1895), ii. 204–7.

WEILL, GEORGES. *L'École Saint-Simonienne, son histoire, son influence jusqu'à nos jours.* Paris, Alcan, 1896. ii+319 pp.

This sequel to *Saint-Simon et son œuvre* continues the history of Saint-Simon's doctrines with his disciples. Weill's account differs from Charléty's in that it considers a larger number of writers and is based in the main on a wide reading of their works. Charléty uses mainly manuscript material drawn from the Archives Saint-Simoniennes. His is the better account of Saint-Simonian psychology, Weill's of Saint-Simonian literature. Thus the two works supplement each other.
Reviews: A. Lichtenberger in *RC*, xlii (1896), 377–9; L. G. Varet in *Rph* (1897), i. 435–7.

WEILL, GEORGES. 'Le Saint-Simonisme hors de France', *RHES*, ix (1921), 103–14.

Saint-Simonism in Belgium, Germany, Sweden, Norway, Russia, Switzerland, England, the United States, and Latin America.

PART III

THE HUMANITARIANS

PIERRE HENRI LEROUX (1797–1871)

ŒUVRES DE PIERRE LEROUX (1825–50). Paris, Sandré, 1850–1. 2 vols.

Begun at an inauspicious moment, this project (which was to have comprised 8 vols.) was never completed.

Werther, traduction nouvelle. Paris, Au Bureau de la Bibliothèque choisie, 1829. Recent eds.: Paris, A l'Enseigne du Pot cassé, 1928 ('Scripta manent'); Paris, J. Tallandier, 1936 (édition de luxe).

De l'Égalité. Paris, Sandré, 1838. Boussac, 1848. xi+272 pp.

Réfutation de l'Éclectisme. Paris, Gosselin, 1839. xviii+351 pp. 2nd ed., Paris, Gosselin, 1841.

De l'Humanité, de son principe, et de son avenir. Paris, Perrotin, 1840, 2 vols. 2nd ed., 1845, 2 vols.

Discours sur la situation actuelle de la société et de l'esprit humain. Paris, Sandré, 1841. 2nd ed., Boussac, 1847. 2 vols.

Malthus et les économistes, ou, y aura-t-il toujours des pauvres? Boussac, 1848. Boussac and Paris (Sandré), 1849. Paris, 1897. 2 vols.

La Grève de Samarez, poème philosophique. Paris, Dentu, 1863–4. 2 vols.

EVANS, DAVID OWEN. *Le Socialisme romantique: Pierre Leroux et ses contemporains*. Paris, M. Rivière (Bibliothèque d'Histoire Économique et Sociale), 1948. 261 pp. Preface by Édouard Dolléans.

Leroux's social idealism and its affinities in Romantic literature

(Sainte-Beuve, George Sand, Victor Hugo). Bibliography, pp. 239–60.

Reviews: In *Bulletin critique 'du livre français*, iii (1948), nos. 8–9; A. Cuvillier in *NL*, 26 August 1948; M. Dommanget in *Paru*, xlv (1948), 78–79; S. de Sacy in *MF*, 1 November 1948, 554; T. Basset in *Political Science Quarterly*, xlii (1948), 1252–3; H. J. Hunt in *French Studies*, iii (1949), 171–4.

EVANS, DAVID OWEN. 'Une supercherie littéraire: le *Werther* français de Pierre Leroux', *RLC*, xviii (1938), 312–25.

The still popular Leroux 'translation' is a rearrangement of the Sevelinges version.

FIDAO-JUSTINIANI, J. E. *Pierre Leroux*. Paris, Librairie Bloud, 1912. 63 pp. ('Philosophes et penseurs'.)

Originally published in the *RDM* (15 May 1906) in response to a request of Brunetière's, this is a study of Leroux's thought at various stages of development.

Review: R. G. in *RC*, lxxiv (1912), 58–59.

GIRARD, HENRI. 'Comment Shelley a été révélé à Victor Hugo: la *Grève de Samarez* de P. Leroux', *RLC*, ii (1922), 369–85.

See also H. Peyre, *Shelley et la France* (Cairo, 1935).

GIRARD, HENRI, 'La Pensée religieuse des romantiques', *RHL*, xxi (1925), 79–97.

The debt of the great Romantic writers to Leroux and the Saint-Simonians.

JANET, PAUL. 'La Philosophie de P. Leroux', *RDM*, clii, 767–88; cliii, 379–406 (1899).

A study of *La Réfutation de l'Éclectisme* and *De l'Humanité*, by a well-known psychologist and life-long admirer of Leroux.

MOUGIN, HENRI. *Pierre Leroux*. Paris, Éditions Sociales Internationales (Socialisme et Culture), 1938. 304 pp.

This study of Leroux's socialism from a Marxist point of view is noteworthy for some excellent pages on the *actualité* of his ideas. Mougin also gives adequate attention to the works of Jules Leroux; he reveals the close team-work done by the two brothers and the part they played in the affairs of the Société des Droits de l'Homme. Selections from Pierre Leroux's writings occupy approximately half the space. Mougin's general conclusions are sound, though his emphasis on Leroux's economics to the exclusion of his idealism seems injudicious.

RAILLARD, CÉLESTIN. *Pierre Leroux et ses œuvres. L'homme, le philosophe, le socialiste.* Châteauroux, 1899. 186 pp.

A curious work, chiefly of interest for the details it gives of Leroux's life at Boussac, where Raillard for some time resided.
Review: A. Lichtenberger in *Rhist*, lxxii (1900), 132.

SALOMON, PIERRE. 'Les Rapports de George Sand et de Pierre Leroux en 1845, d'après le prologue de *La Mare au Diable*', *RHL*, xlviii (1948), 352–8.

Changes made by Leroux in the text of the two introductory chapters of *La Mare au Diable* published in the *Revue Sociale*. Parallels with *Malthus* and *Aux Philosophes*.

STAPFER, PAUL. 'Un Philosophe religieux du XIXᵉ siècle: P. Leroux', in *Questions esthétiques et religieuses*, Paris, Alcan, 1906, pp. 91–143.

The subject of this study, which first appeared in the *Bibliothèque universelle*, xxxvi (1904), is the religious thought of Leroux. It is treated most sympathetically, and with authority.

THOMAS, P. FÉLIX. *Pierre Leroux. Sa vie, son œuvre, sa doctrine. Contribution à l'histoire des idées au XIXᵉ siècle.* Paris, Alcan (Bibliothèque de philosophie contemporaine), 1904. vi + 340 pp.

The best biography, based largely upon Leroux's correspondence but also on oral testimony. The analysis of the doctrine is inferior to Stapfer's: Thomas has been charged with 'editing' Leroux, but it must be admitted that Leroux needs editing.
Reviews: E. Faguet in *Propos littéraires*, v. 41–55; G. L. Duprat in *RIS*, xii (1905), 322; A. Lichtenberger in *Rhist*, lxxxviii (1905), 145.

JEAN REYNAUD (1806–1863)

Notes prises dans les œuvres de Jean Reynaud, 'L'Esprit de la Gaule' et 'Terre et Ciel', par M. M. P. Paris, Rhéa, 1920. 147 pp.

An abridgement, intended for students of theosophy.

Considérations sur l'esprit de la Gaule. Paris, L. Martinet, 1847. 207 pp.

L'Esprit de la Gaule. Paris, Furne, 1864. 373 pp.

Études encyclopédiques. Paris, Furne, 1866–7. 3 vols.

Philosophie religieuse. Terre et Ciel. Paris, Furne, 1854. xiv+ 441 pp.

Lectures variées. Paris, Furne, 1865. 488 pp.

CHEYSSON, E. 'Frédéric le Play et Jean Reynaud', *La Réforme sociale*, xxxvi (1898), 869–85.

Letters to Jean Reynaud from Le Play (1849–57).

CHEYSSON, E. *Jean Reynaud 1806–1863.* Paris, Gauthier-Villars, s.d. (1896). 10 pp.

Reprinted from the *Livre du Centenaire de l'École Polytechnique.*

LEGOUVÉ, E. *Jean Reynaud.* Paris, Charpentier, 1864. 132 pp.

An enthusiastic biography. Legouvé, Reynaud's disciple and friend, considers the determining period in his life to have been that of his collaboration with Leroux on the *Encyclopédie Nouvelle* (1834–41). His writings to the *Revue Encyclopédique* should not be neglected.

MARTIN, HENRI. *Jean Reynaud.* Paris, Furne, 1863. 48 pp.

Reproducing an obituary notice published in *Le Siècle*, followed by a study of *Terre et Ciel* from the *Revue de Paris.*

TAINE, HIPPOLYTE. 'Jean Reynaud, *Ciel et Terre.*' In *Essais de critique et d'histoire*, Paris, Hachette, 1913 (12th ed.), pp. 17–48.

A brief analysis and criticism of Reynaud's metaphysics without reference to its literary interest, on which point see R. Picard, *Le Romantisme social*, pp. 180, 234; A. Viatte, *V. Hugo et les illuminés*, pp. 62–65, 238, 257; J. Vianey, Introduction to the *GÉF* edition of *Les Contemplations.*

Part IV

THE SOCIETARIANS

FRANÇOIS MARIE CHARLES FOURIER (1772–1837)

ŒUVRES COMPLÈTES. Paris, Bureaux de la *Phalange*, 1841–5. 6 vols. 3rd ed., Librairie sociétaire, 1846. 4th ed., Dupont, 1870.

ŒUVRES CHOISIES. Edited by Charles Gide. Paris, Guillaumin, 1890. lvi+232 pp. (Bibliothèque des économistes.) Second ed., Sirey, 1932.

A selection of pages from Fourier of special interest to economists and sociologists. The texts are preceded by a lengthy and judicious introduction. No notes.

Review: G. Bouthoul in *RIS*, xlii (1934), 303–4.

CHARLES FOURIER. *Textes choisis et présentés par Jacques Debû-Bridel.* Geneva and Paris, L.U.F. (Collection des Classiques de la Liberté), 1947. 163 pp.

Théorie des quatre mouvements et des destinées générales. Leipzig (i.e. Lyons, Pelzin), 1808 (anon.). ii+428 pp. Other editions: Bossange, 1840; in *Œuvres complètes*, vol. i.

Fourier's first work.

Traité de l'association domestique-agricole. London and Paris, Bossange, 1822. 2 vols. Republished under the title *Théorie de l'unité universelle*, Paris, 1834, 4 vols; also in *Œuvres complètes*, vols. ii–v.

Contains the essence of Fourier's doctrine.

Le Nouveau Monde industriel et sociétaire, ou Invention du procédé d'industrie attrayante et naturelle, distribuée en séries passionnées. Paris, Bossange, 1829. xvi+664 pp. 3rd ed., 1848. In *Œuvres complètes*, vol. vi.

La Fausse Industrie morcelée, répugnante, mensongère, et l'antidote: l'industrie naturelle, combinée, attrayante, véridique, donnant quadruple profit. Paris, Bossange, 1835–6. 2 vols. Not republished.

ALHAIZA, ADOLPHE. *Charles Fourier et sa sociologie sociétaire.* Paris, Marcel Rivière, 1911. 77 pp.

This brief account of Fourier as founder of Co-operation is chiefly interesting for the first-hand account which it contains of the survival to 1911 of the Fourierist school, with which the author was actively connected, and for its bibliography of Fourierist literature (pp. 71–76).

ARMAND, F., and MAUBLANC, RENÉ. *Fourier.* Paris, Éditions Sociales Internationales (Socialisme et Culture), 1937. 2 vols.

From the Marxist point of view Fourier seems almost a revolutionary. Like the other volumes in the same series the *Fourier* consists of selected texts preceded by an introduction on the author. The texts are in this instance edited with ample notes, a very real service to the reader of Fourier. They illustrate a wider range of aspects of his thought than other selections do: his feminism, for example, is well represented. Vol. i contains an excellent chapter on the economic state of France from 1789 to 1830, another feature of the series. The book is also worth reading for the parallels drawn between Fourier and Marx, Engels, and Lenin, and some remarkable comparisons of the *phalanstère* to certain institutions of the U.S.S.R.

BOURGIN, HUBERT. *Fourier, contribution à l'étude du socialisme français*. Paris, Bellais, 1905. 617 pp. Diss.

Charles Gide has said that this erudite study exhausts the matter of Fourier: life, works, doctrine, and influence. Gide is too modest. It is an extremely thorough and well-documented study of Fourier and his disciples, of their thought and its sources. But there are gaps, e.g. the literary influence, on which Bourgin has extraordinarily little to say. Bibliography, pp. 11–28.

Reviews: E. Fournière in *RSoc*, xlii (1905), 94–96; A. Landry in *RIS*, xiv (1906), 73–4.

FAGUET, ÉMILE. 'Charles Fourier', *RDM*, cxxxvi (1896), 570–94, and in *Politiques et moralistes du XIXᵉ siècle*, vol. ii (Paris, Lecène-Oudin, 1891).

Faguet, a bitter critic of socialism and no authority on the subject, considers Fourier as a parodist of Rousseau.

FLOTTES, PIERRE. *Le Poète Leconte de Lisle*. Paris, Perrin, 1929. 271 pp.

Pp. 43–48, Fourier's influence on *Qaïn*, *La Fontaine aux lianes*, and *Nox*. On the poet's participation in the Fourierist movement see also H. Elsenberg, *Le Sentiment religieux chez Leconte de Lisle* (1909), and Leblond (inf.).

GIDE, CHARLES. *Fourier, précurseur de la Coopération*. Paris, Association pour l'enseignement de la Coopération, s.d. (1924). 203 pp.

Fourier's most brilliant contemporary disciple Charles Gide (André Gide's uncle) was Professor at the Collège de France, where in 1922–3 he gave this course of public lectures on Fourier. Written in an entertaining and witty style, they are concerned (as the title suggests) with the prophetic quality in Fourier and the *actualité* of his ideas. Not all co-operative socialists agree with Gide in viewing Fourier as the founder of the co-operative movement.

Review: A. Ouy in *RIS*, xxxiii (1925), 444–5.

GODIN, J. B. A. 'Les Fouriéristes aux États-Unis', *RSoc*, ix (1889), 602–15.

On this subject see also John Humphrey Noyes, *History of American Socialisms* (Philadelphia, Lippincott, 1870).

JANET, PAUL. 'Le Socialisme au XIXᵉ siècle. La Philosophie de Charles Fourier', *RDM*, xxxv (1 Oct. 1879), 619–46.

An excellent account of Fourier's metaphysics and of his 'reasoned impiety' (important for Leconte de Lisle).

LEBLOND, MARIUS-ARY. *Leconte de Lisle d'après des documents nouveaux*. Paris, Mercure de France, 1906. 478 pp. Chaps. vii, viii, ix.

Leconte de Lisle was an active Fourierist from his coming to Paris in 1845 to June 1848, and published in the *Phalange* a number of poems not collected in his Works. These are here described, with many textual quotations.

PINLOCHE, AUGUSTE. *Fourier et le socialisme*. Paris, Alcan, 1933. 195 pp.

A volume published on the occasion of the centenary of the Condé-sur-Vesgre *phalanstère* and in the midst of the *crise pléthorique* of the 1930s; it consists of an account of the man and his work (pp. 13–59), followed by a series of texts drawn from Fourier, Considerant, Lechevalier, and Pellarin.

Review: in *RIS*, xlii (1934), 407–8.

POISSON, ERNEST. *Fourier*. Paris, Alcan, 1932 (Réformateurs sociaux). 156 pp.

Selected texts from the works of Fourier, with a preface (pp. 1–13) on co-operatives. Poisson, author of *La République co-opérative*, takes a point of view somewhat different from Gide's.

Review: H. Mazel in *MF*, ccxlvi (1933), 180–2.

POMMIER, JEAN. *La Mystique de Baudelaire*. Paris, Belles-Lettres, 1932. vii+201 pp.

Pp. 65–68, the relation of the doctrine of *correspondances* to Fourier's Law of Universal Analogy, on which point see Baudelaire's *Paradis artificiels*, iv, and *L'Art romantique* (Lévy), 316–18.

Review: P. Martino in *RC*, xcix (1932), 305–6.

SEILLIÈRE, ERNEST ANTOINE AIMÉ LÉON, Baron. *Le Mal romantique, essai sur l'impérialisme irrationnel*. Paris, Plon, 1908. lxxvii+396 pp.

Pp. 1–188, 'Le Romantisme des pauvres — Charles Fourier'. Seillière considers Fourier to be the father of Romantic socialism. Subjecting his writings to close psychological analysis, he finds plenty of evidence of 'pathological egotism' and Romantic mysticism. The fact remains, however, that Fourier had relatively little influence upon Romantic literature itself.

Review: L. R. in *RC*, lxvi (1908), 341–2.

VICTOR PROSPER CONSIDERANT (1808–1893)

Considérations sociales sur l'Architectonique. Paris, Librairie phalanstérienne, 1834. xlix+84 pp. 2nd ed., entitled *Description du Phalanstère et considérations sociales sur l'Architectonique*, Paris, 1840. 111 pp. 3rd ed. (same title), Paris, 1848. 111 pp.

Fragments of the forthcoming *Destinée sociale*.

Destinée sociale. Paris, Librairie phalanstérienne, 3 vols. Vol. i, 1834. Vol. ii, 1838. Vol. iii, 1844. 2nd ed., Paris, 1847, 2 vols. 3rd ed., Paris, 1848–9, 2 vols. 4th ed., Paris, 1851, 2 vols.

'Un exposé de la doctrine de Fourier beaucoup plus méthodique, plus clair et plus éloquent que les livres du maître.' Gide, *Fourier*, 147.

Bases de la politique positive. Manifeste de l'École Sociétaire fondée par Fourier. Paris, Librairie phalanstérienne, 1841. iv+120 pp. 2nd ed., Paris, 1842, 218 pp. Another ed., under the title *Bases de la politique rationnelle*, Paris, 1847. 202 pp.

Exposition abrégée du système phalanstérien de Fourier. Paris, Librairie phalanstérienne, 1845. 114 pp. 2nd ed., Paris, 1845. 3rd ed., Paris, 1845. 4th ed., Paris, 1846. 5th ed., Paris, 1848. 6th ed., Paris, 1872. Recent re-edition, Paris, Crès, 1921.

Lectures given at Dijon and published in the *Phalange* in 1840.

Principes du Socialisme. Manifeste de la Démocratie au XIXe siècle. Paris, Librairie phalanstérienne, 1847. 143 pp. Reprinted in *L'Ère Nouvelle*, February 1894.

Reproduces the *Manifeste de la Démocratie pacifique* (1843) and the *Procès de la Démocratie pacifique*.

Le Socialisme devant le Vieux Monde ou le Vivant devant les Morts. Paris, Librairie phalanstérienne, 1848. viii+264 pp. 2nd ed., Paris, 1848. 3rd ed., Paris, 1849. 4th ed., Paris, 1850.

Isambert considers this Considerant's most original work.

BOURGIN, HUBERT. *Victor Considerant, son œuvre.* Lyons, Imprimeries réunies, and Paris, Cornély, 1909. 128 pp.

Not a biography, but a study of the theories and political activities of Victor Considerant, based on a reading of the Fourierist press and of Considerant's *Destinée sociale* and *Bases de la politique positive*. The editor of *Le Phalanstère* (1832–4), *La Phalange* (1836–43 and 1845–9), and *La Démocratie pacifique* (1843–51), who took great pains to persuade people to write his name without an acute accent, was Fourier's chief disciple and publicist.

Review: E. Driault in *Rhist*, ciii (1910), 107.

COIGNET, MADAME C. *Victor Considerant, sa vie et son œuvre*. Paris, Alcan, 1895. 100 pp.

A life of Considerant, by a cousin, and an account of the disastrous experiment in Texas.

Reviews: in *RSoc*, xxii (1895), 765; P. F. Pécaut in *Rph* (1896), i. 96–98.

COLLARD, PIERRE. *Victor Considerant (1808–1893), sa vie, ses idées*. Dijon, L. Marchal, 1910. 297 pp.

This book falls into two parts: Considerant's life, and his ideas. Considerant's own ideas do not assume full prominence in the *Destinée sociale*, which is official documentation on Fourier. Collard gives some account of the Fourierist press and of the Texas experiment.

DOMMANGET, MAURICE. *Victor Considerant, sa vie, son œuvre*. Paris, Éditions Sociales Internationales, 1929. 231 pp.

A well-documented study of Considerant's life and writings and of his relations with contemporary socialists. While he clarified Fourier's doctrine Considerant was not always a thorough-going Fourierist; his ideas changed with the flow of events, particularly after 1848. Dommanget brings out his services to the co-operative movement, his class-consciousness (lacking in Fourier), his feminism (he was the only member of the Assemblée Constituante to support women's suffrage), his republicanism, and his influence on Marx and Engels.

Reviews: H. Sée in *Rhist*, clxi (1929), 367–8; in *RHES*, xvii (1929), 250–1.

RICHARD, GASTON. 'Un Précurseur de l'urbanisme en 1834: Victor Considerant', *RIS*, xlii (1934), 557–61.

Three texts from the *Considérations sur l'Architectonique*.

Part V

PIERRE JOSEPH PROUDHON
(1809–1865)

ŒUVRES COMPLÈTES. Paris, Marcel Rivière, 1923 ff. In course of publication. General editors, C. Bouglé and H. Moysset:

Système des contradictions économiques, ou Philosophie de la misère (Paris, Guillaumin, 1846). Edited by Roger Picard. 1923. 2 vols.

Idée générale de la Révolution au XIXᵉ siècle (Paris, Garnier, 1851). Edited by A. Berthod. 1924. 462 pp.

De la capacité politique des classes ouvrières (Paris, Dentu, 1865). Edited by Maxime Leroy. 1924. 421 pp.

Candidature à la pension Suard. De la célébration du dimanche (Besançon, Bintot, 1839). *Qu'est-ce que la Propriété?* (Paris, Prévot, 1840). Edited by M. Augé-Laribé. 1926. 367 pp.

De la création de l'ordre dans l'humanité, ou principes d'organisation politique (Paris, Prévot, 1843). Edited by C. Bouglé and A. Cuvillier. 1927. 464 pp.

La Guerre et la Paix (Paris, Hetzel, 1861). Edited by H. Moysset. 1927. 514 pp.

Les Confessions d'un révolutionnaire, pour servir à l'histoire de la Révolution de février (Paris, La Voix du Peuple, 1849). Edited by D. Halévy. 1929. 442 pp.

De la Justice dans la Révolution et dans l'Église (Paris, Garnier, 1858). Edited by G. Guy-Grand, G. Séailles, C. Bouglé, and J. L. Puech. 1930–5. 4 vols.

La Révolution sociale démontrée par le coup d'État du 2 décembre (Paris, Garnier, 1852). *Projet d'Exposition perpétuelle* (Paris, Librairie internationale, 1865). Edited by E. Dolléans and G. Duveau. 1936. 386 pp.

Deuxième mémoire sur la propriété (Paris, Prévot, 1841). *Avertissement aux propriétaires* (Paris, Prévot, 1842). *Programme révolutionnaire. Impôt sur le revenu* (Paris, Garnier, 1848). *Le Droit au travail et le droit de propriété* (Paris, Vasbenter, 1848). Edited by M. Augé-Laribé. 1938. 477 pp.

Du principe de l'art et de sa destination sociale (Paris, Lefèvre, 1865). *Galilée. Judith. La Pornocratie ou les femmes dans les temps modernes* (Paris, Librairie internationale, 1875). Edited by J. L. Puech. 1939. 473 pp.

Philosophie du progrès (Brussels, A. Lebègue, 1853). *La Justice poursuivie par l'Église* (Brussels, Office de publicité, 1858). Edited by Th. Ruyssen and J. L. Puech. 1946. 333 pp.

Du principe fédératif et de la nécessité de reconstruire le parti de la révolution (Paris, Dentu, 1863). Edited, with introduction and notes, by Jean Charles-Brun. Paris, Bossard (Collection des Chefs-d'œuvre méconnus), 1921. 222 pp.

Review: in *RC*, lxxxix (1922), 240.

BERTHOD, AIMÉ. *P.-J. Proudhon et la propriété, un socialisme pour les paysans*. Paris, Giard et Brière, 1910. 231 pp. Diss., doctorat en droit.

Light upon a long-neglected aspect of Proudhon: the unity and cohesion of his doctrine. Berthod finds the unifying principle in his views on landed property; his socialism is directed towards peasant proprietorship.

BERTHOD, AIMÉ. 'Les Tendances maîtresses de Proudhon. La balance de l'Égalité et de la Liberté', *RSoc*, xlix (1909), 120–37, 218–38.

The juridic character of Proudhon's doctrine.

BOUGLÉ, CÉLESTIN CHARLES ALFRED. *Proudhon*. Paris, Alcan (Réformateurs sociaux), 1930. 156 pp.

Some forty texts from the writings of Proudhon, illustrating his personal experiences, his ethical and religious views, his political and economic ideas, &c., and preceded by an introduction which deals with his influence.

Review: H. Mazel in *MF*, ccxxiv (1930), 168.

BOUGLÉ, CÉLESTIN CHARLES ALFRED. *La Sociologie de Proudhon*. Paris, Colin, 1911. xviii+333 pp.

Bouglé recognizes in Proudhon a true sociologist despite his individualism and shows that his theory of property needs to be considered in the light of his sociological ideas. The unity of his thought lies in his sociology.

Reviews: B. Combes de Patris in *RScPol*, xxvii (1912), i. 333–4;

G. L. Duprat in *RIS*, xx (1912), 639–41; J. Delvaille in *Rph*, lxxv (1913), 315–18; in *RSoc*, lvii (1913), 274–6.

BOULEN, ALFRED GEORGES. *Les Idées solidaristes de Proudhon.* Paris, Marchal et Godde, 1912. 220 pp.

Proudhon is claimed as an ancestor of Léon Bourgeois. Cf. Bouglé, *Le Solidarisme* (Giard, 1924). It is admitted that in his later writings he veered towards a liberal individualism. An important though exclusive point of view.

Review: E. Chauffard in *RIS*, xx (1912), 641.

BOURGEAT, JACQUES. *Proudhon père du socialisme français.* Paris, Denoël, 1943. 275 pp.

A biography. Written in the atmosphere of 1942, the epilogue claims that Proudhon's day has come, that the old world is done with, and that economics must now take the place of politics. The Bibliography (pp. 247–68) does not list the Rivière edition.

BOURGEOIS, NICOLAS. *Les Théories du droit international chez Proudhon.* Le Fédéralisme et la Paix. Paris, Rivière, 1927. 139 pp.

Proudhon as an apostle of peace by federation. The bulk of the book consists of a study of the *actualité* of Proudhon's doctrine of international law and of the future of federalism. The greatest danger for the future is seen (1927) in the fascist movement.

BROGAN, DENIS WILLIAM. *Proudhon.* London, Hamish Hamilton, 1934. 95 pp.

The only noteworthy study in English is this brilliant Life of Proudhon. Prof. Brogan finds that Proudhon influenced many men in many different ways. He does not propose yet another definition, but concludes that 'it was the influence of his spirit rather than of any consistent body of doctrine that made him important'.

CUVILLIER, ARMAND. *Proudhon.* Paris, Éditions Sociales Internationales (Socialisme et Culture), 1937. 278 pp.

Annotated texts from Proudhon's writings, preceded by an introduction (pp. 9–98) on the economic background and on Proudhon's life, thought, and influence. Cuvillier finds the essence of Proudhon's doctrine in his *mutuellisme* and refuses to consider him a founder of Syndicalism.

Review: in *RIS*, xlv (1937), 427.

DOLLÉANS, ÉDOUARD. *Proudhon.* Paris, Gallimard, 1948. 528 pp.

Dolléans' sympathy with Proudhon has enabled him, with the aid of the unpublished *Carnets*, to write a most understanding study of this great personality and to clarify his intentions in many contentious works. He emphasizes as the key-note the dignity of the individual.

Reviews: B. Voyenne in *La Nef*, xlvi (1948), 38–42: 'Début de l'ère proudhonienne'; G. Duveau in *CIS*, v (1948), 181–3; W. Pickles in *Political Quarterly*, xx (1949), 176–8.

DOLLÉANS, ÉDOUARD, and PUECH, JULES L. *Proudhon et la Révolution de 1848*. Paris, Presses Universitaires de France, 1948. 79 pp.

More interested in social progress than in political evolution, Proudhon, the authors show, at first thought the Republic premature and criticized the Provisional Government and the Assembly. But he was fundamentally a Republican, placing his hope in the people's movement.

DUPRAT, JEANNE. *Proudhon sociologue et moraliste*. Paris, Alcan, 1929. xii+328 pp.

The thesis is that Proudhon tried to found an ethics upon a basis of sociology; that his sociology was inadequate, but that his theory of justice was founded on observation. His study of working-class behaviour is of special interest: he is viewed as a precursor of Durkheim and Lévy-Bruhl. Cf. M. Bernès, *La Morale de Proudhon* (Paris, Alcan, 1904).

Reviews: H. Sée in *Rhist*, clxiv (1930), 187–8; H. Mazel in *MF*, ccxxiv (1930), 164–8; H. Noyelle in *RHES*, xix (1931), 214–15; R. Bastide in *RIS*, xxxviii (1932), 252–5.

GUY-GRAND, GEORGES. *La Pensée de Proudhon*. Paris, Bordas, 1947. vii+234 pp.

Proudhon's works as the expression of 'l'humanisme travailliste' (in Charles Andler's phrase): an intellectual biography accompanied by a critical analysis of his works and concluding with an estimate of the present influence of his constructive thought. Bibliography, pp. 219–25. Index.

Reviews: G. Duveau in *CIS*, v (1948), 181–3; J. Bois in *RSoc*, xxxi (1949), 379–80.

GUY-GRAND, GEORGES. 'Proudhon et Michelet', *Rph*, cxxxviii (1948), 385–408.

Guy-Grand qualifies the parallel drawn by De Lubac between *De la Justice* and the 1847 Preface to Michelet's *Histoire de la Révolution Française*, pointing to Proudhon's unwavering support of immanence against transcendence.

HALÉVY, DANIEL. *La Vie de Proudhon*. Vol. i, Stock, 1948. 448 pp.

Reproducing, enlarged, the author's earlier *La Jeunesse de Proudhon* (Paris, Figuière, 1913), this volume covers the period 1809–38, and for the ensuing ten years follows with Sainte-Beuve's *Proudhon*, annotated with the help of the unpublished *Carnets*.

Review: B. Voyenne in *La Nef*, xlvi (1948), 41–42.

LOSSIER, JEAN G. *Le Rôle social de l'art selon Proudhon*. Paris, Vrin, 1937. 203 pp.

Lossier shows that Proudhon's knowledge of the history of art is sketchy, but that his *Du principe de l'art*, written in 1863, corresponds to a current of ideas which has been a factor in transforming social life and artistic activity. That Romanticism postulates the autarchy of art (p. 58) is a doubtful statement.

Review: A. Ouy in *RIS*, xlvii (1939), 305–6.

LUBAC, R.P. HENRI DE. *Proudhon et le Christianisme*. Paris, Éditions du Seuil, 1945. 318 pp.

Henri de Lubac views Proudhon as a religious spirit in spite of his atheism. His notorious invectives against Catholicism he attributes to the 'folles doctrines' of de Bonald and de Maistre. Tracing the strong Biblical influence in his writings and drawing many parallels with Kierkegaard, he finds in Proudhon's works the elements of a personalist *mystique*. Excellent chapters on his dialectics and on Charity and Justice—the latter, somewhat uncharitable to social romanticism.

Review: B. Voyenne in *La Nef*, xlvi (1948), 39–40.

MARC, ALEXANDRE. *Proudhon*. Paris, Egloff, 1945. 317 pp.

Selected pages from Proudhon's writings, with a preface (pp. 11–52) on their significance to us today. Marc follows Daniel Halévy in associating Proudhon closely with Péguy and with the spirit of the Resistance movement.

Review: B. Voyenne in *La Nef*, xlvi (1948), 38–39: 'la meilleure initiation qu'il soit possible de trouver à l'œuvre de Proudhon.'

MARX, KARL, *Misère de la philosophie*. Paris, Franck, 1847. 179 pp.

An answer (written in French) to Proudhon's *Philosophie de la misère* (1846).

PICKLES, WILLIAM. 'Les Tendances proudhoniennes dans la France d'après-guerre', *RHES*, xxiii (1937), 289–309.

This solidly documented article is full of live interest: of the groups mentioned by Pickles, some have come to the fore in the post-War II period (the review *L'Esprit*, founded in 1932, and the Troisième Force movement started under the same auspices in 1933).

PIROU, GAËTAN. *Proudhonisme et syndicalisme révolutionnaire.* Paris, Rousseau, 1910. xx+422 pp.

Pirou makes a systematic comparison of the thought of Proudhon with Syndicalism. He finds resemblances of detail; in spirit there are important divergences, according to him, between Proudhon and Sorel. For an opposite view see Dolléans, *Proudhon*, pp. 487–509.

Review: R. Picard in *RSoc*, liv (1911), 283–4.

PUECH, JULES L. *Le Proudhonisme dans l'Association Internationale des Travailleurs.* Paris, Alcan, 1907. xix+285 pp. Preface by Charles Andler.

That the Geneva and Lausanne Congresses of the International were swayed by the French delegation, representing largely Proudhon's ideas, and that the influence of Marx dates from the Congress of Geneva, such is the thesis of this book. Puech has shown more fully elsewhere Flora Tristan's part in the conception of this organization.

Reviews: E. Fournière in *RSoc*, xlvii (1908), 280–2; R. Maunier in *RIS*, xvi (1908), 226.

SAINTE-BEUVE, CHARLES AUGUSTIN. *P.-J. Proudhon, sa vie et sa correspondance (1838–48).* Paris, Lévy, 1872. 352 pp. A. Costes, 1947.

A revision of four articles from the *Revue contemporaine* of October–December 1865, comprising a portrait of Proudhon based on his correspondence. The work is unfinished. 'L'admirable livre de Sainte-Beuve' (Dolléans). 'On ne fera jamais meilleure étude sur Proudhon que celle de Sainte-Beuve' (Sorel). See J. Pommier, 'La Genèse du *Proudhon* de Sainte-Beuve', *RHL* (1925), 371–96.

PART VI

THE COLLECTIVISTS

LOUIS JEAN JOSEPH BLANC (1813–1882)

Organisation du travail. Paris, rue Richelieu, 1839. 131 pp. Other editions, 1841, 1845, 1847, 1848.

This work, which first appeared in the *Revue du progrès* of 1839, contains the essential exposition of Louis Blanc's socialism.

Questions d'aujourd'hui et de demain. Paris, Dentu, 1873–84. 5 vols.

GOLLIET, M. *Louis Blanc, sa doctrine, son action.* Paris, Pedone, 1903. 150 pp. Thèse pour le doctorat en droit (Paris).

Louis Blanc considered from the standpoint of political science. The account of his doctrine is based on his speeches and newspaper articles (1832–80) as well as his printed works. Bibliography, pp. 1–2.

RENARD, ÉDOUARD. *La vie et l'œuvre de Louis Blanc.* Toulouse, Imprimerie régionale, 1922. 192 pp. Hachette, s.d. (1924). 331 pp.

A historical study, with bibliography (24 pp.), of Louis Blanc and his political activities. Less than 20 pp. are devoted to his socialism. They lack documentation. It is a misleading statement (p. 22) that Fourier wished to see the powers of the State increased.

Reviews: R. Mauduit in *RIS*, xxxiii (1925), 528; A. Pingaud in *RC*, xci (1924), 135–7; R. Picard in *RHES*, xiv (1926), 138–9.

TCHERNOFF, J. *Louis Blanc.* Paris, Société française de librairie et d'édition (Bibliothèque socialiste), 1904. 112 pp.

This work gives the most adequate analysis of Louis Blanc's ideas which has yet been made. This is followed by an account of his activities in 1848 and of his exile, and a conclusion on his place in the history of nineteenth-century democratic thought. Bibliography, pp. 107–9.

VIDALENC, JEAN. *Louis Blanc.* Paris, Presses Universitaires, 1948. 69 pp.

In the series 'Collection du Centenaire de 1848': a succinct biography. See also G. Duveau in *1848: le Livre du Centenaire* (Éditions Atlas, 1948).

ÉTIENNE CABET (1788–1856)

Voyage et aventures de lord William Carisdall en Icarie, ouvrage traduit de l'anglais de Francis Adams par Th. Dufruit, maître de langues. Paris, Souverain, 1839. 2 vols.

Of this, the original edition, only a few copies were distributed by the anonymous author. Later editions (five from 1840 to 1848) are entitled *Voyage en Icarie, roman philosophique et social.*

Credo communiste. Paris, Prévot, s.d. (1841). 16 pp.

ANGRAND, PIERRE. *Étienne Cabet et la République de 1848*. Paris, Presses Universitaires, 1948. 80 pp.

A most readable account of Cabet's doctrine and of the manner in which the 'spectre of Communism' was stage-managed a hundred years ago.

BOURGIN, GEORGES. 'Documents inédits sur la propagande icarienne de 1840 à 1844', *RSoc*, xlvi (1907), 519–41.

Police reports and other documents from the Archives Nationales, bearing testimony to the activities of the communists in Lyons and other large cities, and to the nervousness of the authorities.

CARRÉ, PAUL. *De la Démocratie au Communisme*. Lille, La Bigot, 1903. 152 pp. Diss.

Attempts to answer the question how Cabet became a Communist (through disillusionment with political democracy, coupled with a strong egalitarian instinct and the influence of four years' exile in England). The bulk of the thesis is an analysis of the *Voyage en Icarie*.

HOLYNSKI, A. 'Cabet et les Icariens', *RSoc*, xiv (1891), 539–50; xv (1892), 40–49, 201–6, 315–21, 449–56; xvi (1892), 292–307.

Holynski, a Russian acolyte, visited the Icarians at Nauvoo (Illinois) in 1854–5. He describes the settlement.

PRUDHOMMEAUX, JULES. *Icarie et son fondateur Étienne Cabet*. Contribution à l'étude du socialisme expérimental. Paris, Cornély, 1907. xl+688 pp. Paris, Rieder, 1926. xl+688 pp. illustrated.

A well-documented and fascinating account of the Icarian community in the United States and of its adventurous history till 1898, when it finally dissolved. Much of the material was gathered in 1904 from surviving members of the Icarians in Illinois and Iowa. Bibliography of Icarian publications, pp. xiii–xl.

Reviews: R. Maunier in *RIS*, xv (1907), 903–4; E. Fournière in *RSoc*, xlvii (1908), 78–81.

CONSTANTIN PECQUEUR (1801–1887)

Économie sociale des intérêts du commerce, de l'industrie, de l'agriculture et de la civilisation en général, sous l'influence des applications de la vapeur; machines fixes, chemins de fer, bateaux à vapeur, &c. Paris, 1836. 2 vols. Paris, Desessart, 1839. 2 vols.

Théorie nouvelle. d'économie sociale et politique, ou Étude sur l'organisation des sociétés modernes. Paris, Capelle, 1842. xxvi + 898 pp.

ANTONELLI, ÉTIENNE. 'Constantin Pecqueur', *RHES*, xviii (1930), 482–504.

A conspectus of Pecqueur's views on the individual and society and an evaluation of his method, based on the *Théorie nouvelle*.

BOURGIN, HUBERT. 'La Doctrine de Pecqueur', *RSoc*, xlv (1907), 407–22, 519–40; xlvi (1907), 30–50, 246–63, 302–14.

The importance of Pecqueur as a channel of transmission from Fourier and Saint-Simon to Marx: one of the best accounts of this thinker.

CUVELIER, ANDRÉE. *La Pensée économique de Constantin Pecqueur*. Lille, 1932. 99 pp. Diss. (Lille).

A critical but superficial review of Pecqueur's religious, social, and political ideas as set forth in the *Théorie nouvelle*, the only one of his works which the author appears to have read.

MAISONNEUVE, LÉON. *Pecqueur et Vidal, contribution à l'histoire du collectivisme en France*. Paris, A. Rousseau, 1898. 132 pp.

Chiefly interesting for its account of Pecqueur's associate François Vidal, this brief study considers the work of both writers as establishing the transition from Utopian to scientific socialism, Pecqueur by his collectivism and Vidal by his social criticism anticipating Marx. The date of Pecqueur's death is wrongly given as 1859. It is hard to agree that the collectivism of Marx differs only in 'le luxe des détails' from his (p. 74).

MALON, BENOÎT. 'Constantin Pecqueur', *RSoc*, vii (1888), 69–79.

An obituary notice by the Editor of the *Revue Socialiste*, containing a brief life of Pecqueur and an excellent summary of his ideas, together with a few pages from his unpublished works.

MARCY, GUSTAVE. *Constantin Pecqueur fondateur du collectivisme d'État (1801–87)*. Paris, Sirey, 1934. x + 268 pp. Diss. (Lille, Faculté de Droit). Preface by B. Lavergne. Bibliography, pp. 259–63.

A thorough and methodical study based partly on unpublished material supplied by Pecqueur's son Eugène Pecqueur and manuscript works from the Chambre des Députés collection. Considering Pecqueur as the earliest collectivist, Marcy shows that his collectivism differs from that of Marx in its spiritualism and its optimism. He refutes Andler's claim that in his works are to be found the outlines of historical materialism and states that what Marx drew from him were elements of his description of the evolution of monopoly capitalism. But in saying 'Enfin, Marx annonce l'avènement du collectivisme par la douleur' (p. 243) he seems to forget an article in *Le Salut du Peuple*.

MARIÉ, JOSEPH. *Le Socialisme de Pecqueur*. Paris, A. Rousseau, 1906. 115 pp. Diss. (Paris).

On two scores Pecqueur is said to anticipate Marx: the socialization of the means of production and distribution, and the theory of labour value. Marié follows Isambert in looking for ethnical explanations of historical movements: according to him, economic determinism is German.

INDEX

L